Everybody Wins

Non-Competitive Games
for
Young Children

JEFFREY SOBEL

ILLUSTRATIONS BY PAULETTE RICH LONG

WALKER AND COMPANY NEW YORK

First published in the United States of America in 1983 by the Walker Publishing Company, Inc.

Published simultaneously in Canada by Thomas Allen & Son Canada, Limited, Markham, Ontario.

ISBN: 0-8027-7237-4

Book design by Laura Ferguson

Library of Congress Catalog Card Number: 82-45220

Printed in the United States of America

10 9 8

ACKNOWLEDGMENTS

Four games excerpted from *The Well-Played Game*, by Bernard De Koven. Copyright © 1978 by Bernard De Koven. Reprinted by permission of Doubleday & Company, Inc.

Excerpts from *The New Games Book*, edited by Andrew Fluegelman. Copyright © 1976 by The Headlands Press, Inc. Reprinted by permission of Doubleday & Company, Inc.

Excerpts from *More New Games*, edited by Andrew Fluegelman. Copyright © 1981 by The Headlands Press, Inc. Reprinted by permission of Doubleday & Company, Inc.

Excerpts from *Giving Form to Feeling*, by Nancy King. Copyright © 1975. Reprinted by permission of Drama Book Specialists (Publishers).

Excerpts from *Learning Through Noncompetitive Activities and Play*, by Bill and Dolores Michaelis. Copyright © 1977. Reprinted by permission of Pitman Learning, Inc., Belmont, California.

Fifteen Games from *The Cooperative Sports and Games Book*, by Terry Orlick. Copyright © 1978 by Terry Orlick. Reprinted by permission of Pantheon Books, Inc., a Division of Random House, Inc.

Eight games adapted from *Winning Through Cooperation*, by Terry Orlick. Copyright © 1978 by Hawkins & Associates, published by Acropolis Books, Ltd., 2400 17th St., NW, Washington, DC 20009.

Excerpts from *Everybody's a Winner*, by Tom Schneider. Copyright © 1976 by Yolla Bolly Press. Reprinted by permission of the publisher, Little, Brown and Company.

Excerpts based on material from *Creative Dramatization* by Katrina Van Tassel and Millie Greimann. Copyright © 1973 Macmillan Publishing Co., Inc. Used by permission of the publisher.

Excerpts and/or adaptations from the following are reprinted by permission as indicated in parentheses:

Games Manual of Non-Competitive Games and *Sports Manual of Co-operative Recreation*, by Jim Deacove (Jim Deacove). *Games*, by Frank Harris (Frank Harris). *For the Fun of It*, by Marta Harrison (Friends Peace Committee). *All Together: A Manual of Cooperative Games*, by Theo Lentz and Ruth Cornelius (Theo F. Lentz). *Every Kid Can Win*, by Terry Orlick and Cal Botteril (Nelson-Hall, Publishers). *Cowstails and Cobras*, by Karl Rohnke (Karl Rohnke).

To our children's children,
in the hope that they will be playing together cooperatively.

✒ CONTENTS

The games and activities in *Everybody Wins* are derived from many sources. Some have had their inception in my own work with young children. Some I invented myself; some are simple cooperative adaptations of traditional games; some are juvenile versions of games for older children and adults. Many have appeared in a different form in other books or were originated by the New Games Foundation of San Francisco, and the origins of these are acknowledged and footnoted below. Many have changed names.

A number of the games and activities are combinations of ideas from more than one author. All are described in my own words and have been adapted and conditioned by my experience in leading children in cooperative—rather than competitive—play. In many cases, they have been reworked so as to be best suited for children from the ages of three to ten.

There are 266 basic games and activities and approximately half again that number of variations. The additional variations that readers are certain to develop in actual play experience will further swell the total.

✒ BE MY PARTNER

LET'S PRETEND

🦢 CHOOSE UP TEAMS

❧ OLD FAVORITES A NEW WAY

❧ SOMETHING TO DO

WHO'S GOT A BALL?

🍃 GUESS WHAT?

🍃 WHAT'LL WE PLAY NOW?

❧ LET'S PLAY QUIETLY

🍃 FOR THE FEW OR THE MANY

1. Deacove, Jim. *Games Manual of Non-Competitive Games.* Perth, Ont., Canada: Jim Deacove, 1974.
2. ———. *Sports Manual of Co-Operative Recreation.* Perth, Ont., Canada: Jim Deacove, 1978.
3. De Koven, Bernard. *The Well-Played Game: A Player's Philosophy.* Garden City, N.Y.: Anchor Books/Doubleday, 1978.
4. Fluegelman, Andrew. *More New Games.* Garden City, N.Y.: Dolphin Books/Doubleday, 1981.
5. ———. *The New Games Book.* Garden City, N.Y.: Dolphin Books/Doubleday, 1976.
6. Harris, Frank. *Games.* Philadelphia: Frank Harris, 1976.
7. Harrison, Marta. *For the Fun of It.* Philadelphia: Philadelphia Yearly Meeting of the Religious Society of Friends, Peace Committee, 1975.
8. King, Nancy. *Giving Form to Feeling.* New York: Drama Book Specialists (Publishers), 1975.
9. Lentz, Theo, and Cornelius, Ruth. *All Together: A Manual of Cooperative Games.* St. Louis: Peace Research Laboratory, 1950.
10. Michaelis, Bill, and Michaelis, Dolores. *Learning Through Noncompetitive Play Activities.* Palo Alto, Calif.: Education Today Co., 1977.
11. The New Games Foundation, San Francisco.
12. Orlick, Terry. *The Cooperative Sports and Games Book.* New York: Pantheon, 1978.
13. ———. *Winning Through Cooperation.* Washington, DC: Acropolis Books, Ltd., 1978.
14. ——— and Botterill, Cal. *Every Kid Can Win.* Chicago: Nelson-Hall, 1975.
15. Rohnke, Karl. *Cowstails and Cobras.* Hamilton, MA: Project Adventure, 1977.
16. Schneider, Tom. *Everybody's a Winner.* Boston: Little, Brown & Co., 1976.
17. Van Tassel, Katrina, and Greimann, Millie. *Creative Dramatization.* New York: Macmillan, 1973.

🦢 INTRODUCTION

What is cooperative play?

Cooperative play consists of games and activities that the participants play together, rather than against one another, just for the fun of it. Through this kind of play, we learn teamwork, trust, and group unity. The emphasis is on total participation, spontaneity, sharing, the joy of play, acceptance of all players, playing our best, changing rules and boundaries to suit the players, and recognizing that *every* player is important. We don't compare our differing abilities and past performances, we don't emphasize winning and losing, results and standings.

Competitive games often result in isolating some players in favor of creating stars. Practices, uniforms, waiting a turn, specialized skills, strict rules, equipment, coaches, spectators, and choosing teams—where the worst player is chosen last— have no part in cooperative play. Instead, we compare how we do to our own past performances, and not to how the other players are doing. We learn how to accept our mistakes, how to be supportive with the mistakes of other players. Since each player's role is important, no one is isolated.

Because teams are for the moment, and sides are changed often throughout this kind of play, all of the players in a cooperative game really represent one total team. No one person's ability is as important as the simple fact of participating and having fun together. This kind of activity conveys an important message: you are okay just the way you are; we accept you. No one is ever singled out as being the best or the worst, chosen last or made to play the least popular position because he or she does not measure up to the abilities of the others. The players are more important than the game; we care about each other, not about the strict interpretation of rules and traditions.

Games can foster good traits or bad ones. Competitive play leads to competition in other aspects of living; cooperative play leads to a wider cooperation with others. In a competitive game, a player reaches the objective—winning—only if the other player or players fail; everyone but the winner ends up as loser, and the winner can't help but enjoy everyone else's loss. Traditional competition is a necessary part of life, but it must include the element of failure; cooperative play provides a needed counterbalance to the unavoidable competition.

It is time to change our concept of "competition." There is competition in some of the games in this book, but not the kind that ends with teams or individuals hating each other. The competition in these games comes mainly from within one's own self, with players trying to do their best without regard to who is winning. In many, the players switch sides so often during the play that they can't get angry at the other team—they know they will eventually *be* on the other team. It is the players' effort that is judged, not the winning. In cooperative play, we have fun first, and emphasize competition when players are ready for it—when they have come to enjoy the game and have learned the fundamental skills.

Many people eliminate themselves from sports at an early age, never to return, because they have been turned off by too much competition. Children should play games that give them confidence and a feeling of worth, not a sense of rejection because they are not as athletically adept as some others. There is no doubt in my mind that there is a need for more cooperative play in the lives of most children. Children learn through their play; in traditional games they learn that they must win to be a worthy person; through cooperative play the child learns to share in the fun of an activity with others—that the experience itself is rewarding.

"Adults have taken over children's sports as if schoolyard games were no longer possible," say Thomas Tutko and William Bruns in their book, *Winning is Everything and Other American Myths.* Children's sports have often been professionalized to such a point that there are only a few places where the kids can go just to have fun. Coaches are everywhere, eager for trophies. They place their expectations on the children—and take all the fun out of the game.

If our children play cooperatively from an early age, by the time they are adults they will have learned the value of cooperation, and society as a whole might well be in better shape.

There are games and activities in this book, all played cooperatively. Although some of them have an element of competition, *all* have the element of cooperation. They are for all children, from three to 103 years old, but the majority are for the grade school and preschool youngster—from ages three to ten. With every description, the most applicable age range is given, although if your players do not fit into a particular group, try the game anyway.

With every game, the players will be learning more about cooperation, sharing, getting along with their playmates. But you don't have to tell them this. They will be having such a good time, they won't even care!

✎ FOR THE LEADER

In these games, most of the direction of the play comes from the players themselves. The pace must change with their needs. If you, the leader, see that your players are starting to tire, simply change to another game or take a short break.

Change is an important word for the leader, as well as for the players. We change boundaries, rules, equipment, the number of players, sides—anything that will help us have more fun. If a game does not flow, we can try to alter it by asking for suggestions, or we can simply go on to another game. Try to allow yourself and your players the chance to be creative, innovative and spontaneous through change; you can even change a game so much that you have invented a brand-new one. Anything is possible as long as you are having fun and playing safely. After certain rules for safe play are securely in everyone's mind, and after the game is flowing by itself, then you, the leader, can join in the fun and still maintain order— and show the kids that there is still a bit of the child left in you!

To start a new game, the leader should get all the players grouped together, quiet and, if possible, sitting down. Then, using your own style, whether it be humor, a story, or what- ever, give a very short explanation of the game you are about to play. Stress safety, the boundaries, describe the equipment if any, and give the rules of the game. Then start the game at a slow pace to allow the children to learn as they play. If there are many rules and explanations, they can be added as the game progresses, starting with only the most basic. The children should learn through playing the game.

If any choosing of teams, partners, etc., is required, I suggest you use the cooperative forms described in this book.

At the beginning of the play period there may be a few children who are hesitant about playing, for one reason or another. Treat such children carefully, or you may lose them. Have some of the others try to coax a hesitant child to play, or do it yourself, but don't push. Let him or her sit and watch the others. Usually, after a short time the reluctant child will join in —possibly with a little more coaxing and assuredly with a lot more enthusiasm than initially.

The end of a game may be a long time off or it may be right around the corner. If the children are having fun you might play the game again, but I suggest that you change to another game if any of your players show resistance, before more get tired of what you are presently playing. End the game before it ends itself.

We play these games and take part in these activities to allow our children to have fun while learning to cooperate, but children will be children. Most of the time the games will go smoothly, but if one doesn't flow, don't take it personally—just change to another game. Allow your children freedom in their play, and they will grow.

Be My Partner

🌱 GIBBERISH

All ages

The players carry on a conversation with their partners without using words. They have to make up sounds that make no sense to them and have the conversation that way. If the cavemen and cavewomen could do it, so can we.

🌱 BODY PARTS CONVERSATION

All ages

For this activity, the players carry on a conversation with their partners without talking, using different parts of their bodies to communicate. Everyone will be amazed at what an elbow or a belly button can have to say.

🌱 ECHO

All ages

One player starts by saying a word, and then the other player repeats the word. They go back and forth with the same word. That's all there is to it. Continue this until one player wants to stop—and that's the tricky part. How does the first player get the second one to stop when he or she is repeating everything the first one says? I guess the first player will have to be quiet for a very, very long time. Maybe all day.

🌱 TOGETHER

All ages

The players choose partners. The two run, skip, hop, bounce, do anything that partners can do together. For instance, holding one hand and spinning around like a top, Or one partner becomes a ball that the other bounces around the play area. It doesn't matter what they do, as long as they do it together.

VARIATION

Try this with groups of more than two partners and multiply the fun.

❧ PARTNER EXERCISES

All ages

Here are some unusual exercises that are fun to do and great for the body. The secret is to do them with a partner.

The partners stand facing one another with arms extended full length and hands on the other person's shoulders. Now they try to push each other into the ground, applying gentle pressure at first, increasing it for a while, and then reducing the pressure again.

Here's another exercise that is fun. While the players face their partners, have them extend opposite hands and place them palm to palm. Now both press hard. They don't try to push the other over, but just press as hard as possible.

VARIATIONS

Wheelbarrow: One player places both hands on the floor or ground. The other holds the first player's feet, keeping them off the ground. Both players move forward in this position.

Push-Pull: For this exercise, both players face each other and hold hands. Their right feet are back behind them. Now both push and pull back and forth with their arms.

Partner Balance: Both partners stand side by side with right foot against right foot. Both lean away from each other while holding right wrists. The players pull each other as they increase the pressure, but they maintain their balance while they do.

Partner Pull-ups: One player lies face up. The other straddles him or her, facing and holding both hands. The standing player pulls the other up and down.

Tandem Push: Both players lie on their backs with their feet pressing against those of their partner. Taking turns, they push and pull their feet backward and forward as though they were pedaling a bike.

❧ PARTNER BALANCING

All ages

Materials needed: A large rubber ball; a flat board, $2'' \times 3'$ (optional); a small boat (optional); an orange (optional); blocks (optional)

Two partners face each other and balance a ball between their bodies without using their hands (younger players can use a hand where needed). Hands can be at the players' sides, or partners can hold hands.

VARIATIONS

Try having three, four, or more players balancing one or more balls.

Try substituting blocks or other objects for the ball.

Have very advanced players try to balance the objects on some part of their bodies or heads.

Two players hold a flat board and balance various objects, such as an orange or a tennis ball, on it. Let them try walking around, or even over obstacles while they do it.

If you are outdoors and very courageous, use an egg.

⚑ ADD-A-LINK

All ages

The players start with partners, standing side by side with their elbows linked. When the leader calls "Add-a-Link," each pair links up with another pair. But only two pairs may link up at one time. In the next round, four and four link up, until all the players are in one long chain.

⚑ COOPERATIVE SEESAW

Nursery school and kindergarten

Needed: See below

Practically everyone loves a seesaw, and there are several ways to create a good one. One method is for the players to make an original "seesaw sit-up" (see below) without using any equipment. Or we could cheat a bit and use *some.* Use almost anything for this that doesn't sit flat on the floor. One possibility is to get an old tire, balance it on the center of a thick piece of wood, and seesaw back and forth.

VARIATIONS

Get a few long boards, one thicker than the others. Crisscross them, using the top one as the seesaw. (Watch out for splinters in the players' sitting area!)

Jumping Jacks: When you have a secure teeter-totter, have a player jump up and come down on one side of it, sending the other player up in the air like a jumping jack.

❧ SEESAW SIT-UP

Nursery school and kindergarten

This seesaw can be used anywhere, since the players *are* the seesaw. All each needs is a friend to play with.

This is basically the traditional sit-up, but done with a partner. The partners sit facing one another, one with legs spread apart, the other between the partner's ankles and with his or her legs around the partner's waist. They hold hands and seesaw back and forth, each going all the way down until his or her back touches the floor.

VARIATION

Combine two seesaws to make a Quadro Seesaw. For this two players form a seesaw and two more make another one across the first pair's legs, at right angles. Then each pair seesaws up and down alternately.

❧ FRIENDSHIP

Nursery school and kindergarten

This one comes from an old song. All we have done is added a movement.

Partners stand side by side or back to back. They sing:

Friendship, friendship
Just a perfect blendship
When other friendships are forgot
Ours—will still be hot.
Da-da-da da-da
Hep hep hep.

Da-da-da da-da
Hep hep hep.

With each "hep," the players bump hips (or behinds) with their partners. Sing as long as the players' voices and their derrières hold out.

❧ LEAD ON

Nursery school and kindergarten

Needed: Obstacles—see below

Set up obstacles in the play area—"mountains," etc. Have the players choose partners. Then they pretend that they are on a long journey and that one of the pair has been temporarily blinded and must be led to safety, over or under any obstacles. When the pair finally make it to safety at the end of the play area, the blinded player can see again, but the sighted player is now blinded. So they switch places and go back again, until everyone is home and both players can see.

VARIATION

Try using some of the other players as obstacles to be avoided.

❧ USE YOUR PARTNER

Nursery school and kindergarten

One partner pretends to be an object that the leader calls out, such as an airplane, a banana, or a chair. Then the second player uses that partner in any way she or he likes. Remind the players to be gentle with their friends.

Then reverse the roles, so that everyone gets a turn to use and be used.

❧ SIAMESE ROLLING

Nursery school through first grade

It's fun to roll down a hill, on a mat, on the lawn, or just about anywhere. It's even more fun to do it with a partner.

First, get everyone in the mood by simply having them roll around like a log on the ground. Then have one, two, or more players roll another player along.

Now try it this way: Have two players lie head to head lengthwise, holding hands. They are to roll as a team, without letting go. If they can master this, let them try to roll feet to feet, with soles together.

❧ MIRRORS AND SHADOWS

Nursery school through first grade

Mirror, mirror on the wall
Who's the fairest of them all?

That's what the wicked queen in *Snow White* says. Peter Pan lost his shadow, and Wendy had to sew it back on. Let's play Mirrors and Shadows.

Choose partners for Mirrors and decide that one will be the mirror and must copy everything his or her partner does. The players must face one another, but they can be standing still or moving around, as long as they stay together in the "mirror" position.

In Shadows, one player is *behind* his or her partner, following every move.

Mirrors and shadows as objects copy us; in this activity we copy a friend, which is much more fun.

❧ PUPPET ON A STRING

Nursery school through first grade

One player is the puppet on the ground, unable to move. Along comes the puppeteer, who brings the puppet to life with pretend strings. The puppeteer pulls the strings, and the puppet responds to every tug. Allow everyone a chance to be the puppeteer as well as to be the puppet.

🖉 Honk, Honk

Kindergarten through second grade

Practically every teenager these days learns how to drive a car, but even the very young can drive in this activity.

The players choose partners. One is the car, the other the driver. The "cars" get down on their hands and knees, and the drivers climb aboard! Off they go, honking their horns. (If the driver is too heavy for the car, tell him or her to keep both feet on the ground.)

VARIATION

This activity is similar, but here the other player is not a car but a puppet. Or one player can be a mad scientist and the other a monster, to be directed by a master.

🖉 Someone Else's Space

Kindergarten and up

The players stand close to their partners and move their arms in the space that is not being used by the other. Both players will be moving their arms at the same time, but they will not be touching each other as they move.

VARIATION

Try having the players move their entire bodies into the other players' spaces, or have many players moving about but not touching one another.

🖉 Leaps into Small Spaces

Kindergarten and up

For this activity it is important for the players to know where their partners plan to go. After playing together for a while they will become familiar with their partner's moves and be able to carry out the activity successfully.

Two players stand at opposite ends of the play area. Then they run toward one another and leap. The object is to land very close together but not touch.

Now try it with four players coming from different points in the play area. As the players run toward one another, have them do it slowly at first and increase their speed when they become more familiar with their partner's moves. When they get good at it, increase the number of participants.

✍ FINISHING WHAT SOMEONE STARTS

Kindergarten and up

One player begins any imaginary activity—it can be anything from building a snowman to washing a dog. At some point the player stops and his or her partner finishes this pretend activity.

Then have the players switch roles and have the other one start an activity. It's all about playing together.

✍ ACTION REACTION

Kindergarten and up

One player does an action or makes a sound that requires some sort of response. The second player responds with another action. Then the first player starts a new action that requires a response, or, alternatively, responds to the second's action. This can keep the activity going for a very long time.

✍ SOUND AND MOVEMENT CONVERSATION

Kindergarten and up

One player starts by making some sounds that make no sense at all. That player's partner responds with a movement to these sounds, showing how they make him or her feel. Then the second player makes sounds, and the first player responds. They are having a sound and movement conversation.

VARIATION

Try this with three, four, or more players.

❧ DRESS ME

Kindergarten and up

Needed: Large, old shirt

One player wears an old shirt that is very big, and holds hands with a partner. They must continue to hold hands while two other players try to take the shirt off the first person and put it on the second. They'll have to do this over the partners' heads and their connected hands and arms. The shirt will be turned inside out during this process, but that's all right. Continue this dressing and undressing until everyone has had a chance.

❧ ME SWITCH

Kindergarten and up

To start, the players learn three simple hand signals. One could be arms crossed on the chest; another could be hands angled over the eyes; the third, one bent arm pointing up and the other hand touching the opposite elbow. Use these signals, or make up your own. Just be sure the players learn all three signals before starting.

Once the players have practiced the three signals, the action begins. Two players face each other. One says "Me switch." At the time this is said, or as close after it as possible, both players show one of the three signals. The object is for both players to show the same signal. If they do, they win. However, if they show different signals, the player who was silent now says "Me switch," and once again both players show a sign. The action continues back and forth with the players taking turns saying "Me switch" until they make the same signal. The faster the action the better!

❧ AURA

Kindergarten and up

Two players stand facing one another, one arm extended and pressing the partner's palm. Both players close their eyes. Now they drop their hands to their sides, turn around once in place, and try to relocate their partners' outstretched palms. Once they do, they open their eyes.

On the second round, they touch palms with their eyes closed, turn around in place *twice,* and then try to find their partners' hands. The next time, they turn three times, and so on. Each time it gets to be more of a challenge.

🦢 EGG TOSS

Kindergarten and up

Get enough uncooked eggs so that you have one for every two players. The players line up in two lines, partners facing, a few feet apart. At a signal, all the players on one side throw their eggs to their partners. If the egg breaks, the pair is eliminated. Have the partners who still remain step farther apart each time they throw their eggs at the leader's signal. Continue until everyone has been eliminated in an egg bath.

Let all the partners shake hands after the activity is over to share the yolk of it all.

🦢 ALI BABA AND THE FORTY THIEVES

Kindergarten and up

Two players stand facing each other a few feet apart. One of the players sings the words "Ali Baba and the forty thieves" to any made-up tune, at the same time doing a hand movement, such as clapping. When the singer is finished, the second player repeats the song and the motions exactly; at the same time, the first player sings the phrase again and does something different with his or her hands—hitting one arm with the opposite hand, for example.

For the next round, the second player must copy this second set of movements, along with continuing to sing, and so on, with both players singing "Ali Baba and the forty thieves" over and over, each doing a different hand movement. The activity can go on forever, or at least until one of the players forgets the line.

VARIATION

With the players in a circle, the first player starts, and the second player repeats what the first player did. Then the first player starts another motion while the third player in the circle does what the second player just finished. Each act goes around the circle, originating with the first player. Finally the first player stops, and one at a time the players in the circle come to a stop. It's like singing a round.

❧ PARTNERS UP

Kindergarten and up

Two partners sit back to back with their elbows linked. Now, without letting go, they try to stand up. It's harder than it sounds. For a "front up," both partners sit facing and holding hands with their legs straight in front of them and their feet touching the partner's. They must stand up without letting go.

VARIATIONS

Try this with two, three, four, or more players in a circle, either back to back or feet to feet.

Once both players of "back up" are up, and with their elbows still linked, one player leans forward, lifting the other off the ground and giving his or her body a gentle stretch.

In "front up," try stopping halfway up, with both partners holding hands, backs straight, and knees at right angles. Hold that position for a short while.

❧ SITTING PARTNERS

Kindergarten and up

Needed: Music (optional)

The players form two circles, one inside the other, so that each player has a partner in the other circle. Once everyone has a partner, each circle starts to move in opposite directions. When the signal is given by the leader, everyone runs to his or her partner, takes hold of both hands, and they sit down together.

VARIATION

This game can be played like Musical Chairs, with the players moving to the music and then running to their partners when the music stops.

❦ COOPERATIVE FLOATING

Kindergarten and up

This is a good activity for anyone learning to swim. It is to be played in a pool or other safe swimming area.

The players choose partners. With both players in the water, they hold hands—both hands. One lies down in the water, still holding the partner's hands. Now the standing partner pulls the other through the water, and the other practices floating, kicking, getting his or her head wet, or whatever else they want to do.

After a while the partners switch places, so that each player has a turn at both positions. See how much fun and how easy swimming can be?

❦ PEOPLE TO PEOPLE

Kindergarten and up

Everyone finds a partner and stands next to him or her. The leader stands in the middle and starts to sing the words "people to people," over and over until everybody is singing along. When everyone is really rocking to the beat, the leader changes the words to include a body part, such as "knee to knee." At this time all the players touch knees with their partners. Then the leader sings another body part, such as "nose to nose," and the partners touch noses.

The leader continues to sing out body parts, ending finally with "people to people." At this time, all the players race to find a new partner, and the new leader is that one player who could not find one. If there is an even number of people playing, try this game with partner groups of more than two, with a new leader chosen randomly each time. The game continues as before, with the leader setting the pace.

❧ EYE-TO-EYE CONTACT

Kindergarten and up

Everyone moves around the play area, doing whatever they want, until the leader says "Freeze." At this moment, each player makes eye contact with another—even one far away—and holds it. When everyone has made eye contact, they go over and meet the player they are looking at. Then they perform some activity together, keeping their eyes on one another's the whole time.

❧ BARLEY BREAK

Kindergarten and up

Set up two end zones, which are the safety areas, with the running field between them.

Partners, holding hands, run from one safety area to the other when the leader calls to them to do so; as they do, the player who is "it" tries to tag them as they cross. If a player is tagged, his or her partner can run alone while the tagged person helps "it" catch the others as they cross.

When both partners have been caught, they hold hands again and help to catch the others running free. The game ends when everyone is finally caught.

❧ BUMP

First grade and up

Needed: Tube sock or old towel; Schmerltz (optional)

Three people play together, and of course you can have as many groups of three as you want.

One player stands a short distance away from the other two, who stand facing each other. The first player throws a knotted tube sock, or a knotted towel, toward the partners, and they attempt to get it without using their hands. They do it by leaning against each other and catching the sock between their bodies.

If they can't catch the sock, the thrower tries again, until they finally succeed.

Then the two catchers walk to the line where the thrower stands, holding the sock between their bodies. The players change position and the game continues until everyone has had a chance as thrower. (After this, the players will be ready for the big leagues!)

VARIATION

Try it with a Schmerltz (see page 72)

⚘ LEMMNE STICKS

First grade and up

Needed: Cut broomsticks, about 18" long; record player, piano, or tape player

This activity has been called Lemmne Sticks, Lumni Sticks, and Lummey Sticks. Whatever it's called, the players are sure to have fun.

Give each player two pieces of broomstick, cut to about eighteen inches in length. Everyone finds a partner. Now spread the partners out so there is plenty of room between them, and have them sit Indian fashion on the floor facing one another. Each player holds a stick in each hand.

Now the players experiment with their sticks by hitting them on the ground and against their partner's sticks. They can hit right stick to right stick, then left to left, then right to left. Allow the players to play around with the Lemmne Sticks so they get to know their moves as well as their partner's.

Now the leader is going to play some music while the players try to synchronize hitting the sticks with the music. Try to get all the players to hit the same places at the same time. Experiment with this; it's a lot of fun.

⚘ BOFFING

First grade and up

Needed: rolled-up newspapers or foam sticks

Boffers are soft swords. The original boffer was made by The New Games Foundation out of polyethylene foam, but a rolled-up newspaper will do just fine.

Roll up a newspaper, not too thick, and start dueling with a partner. The whack of one sword against another—or against a body—can be deafening, but it doesn't hurt. Just be sure to keep the action away from the eyes.

Have plenty of extra papers on hand for those swords that can't take the punishment.

Let's Pretend

❧ SNAKE IN THE GRASS

All ages

This game works just as well on a carpeted floor as on the grass.

Define a limited area, outside of which the runners cannot go. One player is "it" and crawls around hissing like a snake, trying to touch the others running around in the "snake pit"— the playing area. When a player is tagged by the snake, that player becomes a snake as well and must try to tag the others. Eventually everyone is crawling and hissing.

VARIATION

Have half the players start off as snakes and the other half as people. Every time a player is touched by a snake, they switch positions. Thus the game can go on for a very long time— maybe forever.

In this version, it is not necessary to choose players to be snakes. Ask for volunteers; it usually works out to be fairly even.

❧ RUBBER BAND

All ages

Have everyone hold hands and form a circle (if possible). Then have them pretend the circle is a rubber band and tell all the players to stretch it as far as it can go without breaking. (If it breaks, just put it back together by holding hands once again.) Now have the rubber band go inward; all the players walk toward the center of the circle until they meet.

Repeat this until the circle breaks. Then form small groups of children holding hands, which are little rubber bands, and start all over again with stretching. Try shooting your rubber bands across the play area.

❧ SEAT TRAIN

All ages

All the players line up behind one another. They spread their legs apart, and the first player in line crawls through all the legs and sits at the end of the line. The next player does the same and sits behind the first. Everyone does the same until they are all sitting in line, in a "train."

VARIATION

Try having the first player in line run to the end of the line and sit down. All the rest of the players follow when it is their turn, until everyone is seated in train formation. Then the first player can once again run to the end, but stand there this time.

ꙮ BARNYARD

All ages

It is evening, and feeding time on the farm. The cows and the ducks are ready to eat, but the cows want to eat with the other cows, and the ducks want to eat with the other ducks. So the problem is to have each animal find its own kind.

Ask your players to choose to be either a cow or a duck, but not to tell anyone which they have chosen. A cow says "Moo" and a duck says "Quack." Since it is dark on the farm, all the players close their eyes and crawl around, mooing or quacking as they go. When one meets another who is making the same sound, they hold hands and crawl around together; finally all the cows are together and so are all the ducks. Then everyone pretends to eat.

VARIATIONS

For the very young, have the players start with their eyes open. If necessary, let all the players be the same animal at first. Then make the game a little harder by dividing the group into two different ones.

Choose about six different kinds of animals. Assign them to the various players in a whisper; there should be at least two of each kind. As the game begins, each player makes his or her own animal's sound and tries to find his or her "mate."

🪶 TRAIN

Nursery school and kindergarten

Here's an oldie that's still a lot of fun for everyone.

All the players form a line with their arms on the shoulders or around the waist of the person in front of them. The first player in line is the engine, the one at the end is the caboose, and the others are the cars of the train. "Toot, toot!" and "Chugga, chugga!" are usual noises coming from this train.

Now they move, without letting go.

The little ones love this game, coming, going, or just playing around.

🪶 THREAD THE NEEDLE

Nursery school and kindergarten

Have two players hold hands—they are the needle. Then one player, who is the thread, goes through the eye of the needle. It's threaded! Let everyone try each position.

🪶 INGREDIENTS

Nursery school and kindergarten

The circle of players is the mixing bowl in which all the ingredients will be mixed. One player is chosen to be the flour, a few others the eggs, another the milk. Add as much as you like and ask each player to mix in the mixing bowl with the other ingredients. The cake could even be a birthday cake, with some of the players being candles. All you have to figure out then is how to ignite the candles!

🪶 WASHING MACHINE

Nursery school and kindergarten

The play area is our huge washing machine, and all the players are clothes. The leader instructs the players to choose one piece of clothing they would like to be and then puts them through all the cycles: wash, soak, spin, rinse, and any others the leader or the players can think of. After the clothes are fully washed, hang them out to dry, or place them in the dryer for a spin. Have all the clothes really mix together for a great wash and dry.

🖐 EGG BEATER

Nursery school and kindergarten

The leader is the egg beater and leads the players verbally through this activity. The players are the eggs in a pretended giant mixing bowl. Mix up those eggs and have all of them swish together, first slowly and then faster, as the egg beater increases speed until all the eggs are in one smooth glob at the bottom of the mixing bowl. Then pour the eggs into the frying pan, which is, of course, very hot; the eggs will jump around on the pan.

🖐 OBSTACLE PEOPLE

Nursery school and kindergarten

Some of the players spread around the play area and make themselves into obstacles. They can be a bridge to be climbed over, a tunnel to be climbed through, or anything else they can think up. The rest of the players must crawl under, over, around, and through these obstacles. After everyone has navigated all the obstacles, they all switch places so that everyone gets a chance at both positions.

🖐 OCTOPUS

Nursery school and up

This game is *the* favorite of my nursery school and kindergarten classes. Each day when the kindergarten children walk into our playroom, they chant "Oc-to-pus, Oc-to-pus, Oc-to-pus" or "Pus-pus-pus." Then, when I ask them what they would like to play, the answer comes in loud, ringing tones, "OCTOPUS!"

All the players cross back and forth from one side of the play area to the other when the leader calls "Cross," trying not to be tagged by the octopus—one player running around in the middle of the "ocean." When the octopus touches a running player, the tagged person becomes a tentacle, frozen in his or her tracks and able to move only the arms. As the fish cross back and forth, the tentacles try to help the octopus catch them—but only by reaching out with their arms.

Soon the entire ocean will be swarming with tentacles, and the octopus will have an easy time of it; finally everyone will be a tentacle. That's the time to choose a new octopus and play again.

VARIATION

For more action for everyone, let the tentacles move freely to catch the fish.

🍃 Dancing in the Rain

Nursery school and kindergarten

The players dance while the leader tells them what the weather conditions are. Depending on whether it is sunny or cloudy, snowy or rainy or windy or any weather the leader decides, they change their movements.

🍃 Fish Gobbler

Nursery school and kindergarten

A fish gobbler is a giant fish that eats little fish. In this game all the players are little fish who run back and forth from the ship to the shore trying not to get in the grasp of the fish gobbler, a player chosen by the leader.

When the leader calls "Ship," all the players run toward one end of the play area; at the call of "Shore" they run in the opposite direction. The call of "Fish gobbler" means the giant fish is coming. The only way to be safe from the fish gobbler is to lie down on your belly and be touching someone else at the same time. If the fish gobbler tags you before you are lying down and touching someone else, you too become a fish gobbler.

For the very young, introduce this game with all rules the same except that at first the leader is the fish gobbler and does not catch anyone. This gives the players a better chance to enjoy the game.

❧ NAME TRAIN

Nursery school through first grade

Everyone stands in a circle, and the leader chooses one player to be the locomotive. This player enters the circle and proceeds to "chugga-chugga" and "choo-choo" around the inside of it. Then the locomotive approaches one of the players on the circle and says, "Hi, I'm Jeff" (at least that's what I would say; you would use your own name). The player answers by saying his or her name. The locomotive thereupon breaks into a cheer for this player. For example, if the player's name is "Rich," the locomotive would jump up and down and shout "Rich! Rich! Rich! Rich!"

After the cheer, Rich becomes the locomotive and Jeff becomes the caboose, and both "chugga-chugga" up to another player in the circle and introduce themselves to this person. Upon learning the name, both Jeff and Rich give a loud cheer for him or her, and the game continues until everyone has been introduced and has been cheered by the train of players.

❧ SPINNING TOPS

Nursery school through first grade

Practically everyone loves to spin and spin around until they are too dizzy to stand.

In this activity all the players are tops. They start by lying on their sides, as tops do when they are not spinning. Then they jump up and spin around furiously. They will bump into each other as they spin, but that's fun, too, as long as they are gentle.

VARIATION

It's amazing how easily a top turns into an airplane. It stops spinning and holds its arms out to start flying! The play area becomes an airport, with all the airplanes carefully flying around to avoid collisions.

🖎 BALLOONS

Nursery school to first grade

Tell the group that they are all balloons and that they have no air inside of them, so they must all lie motionless on the ground or on the floor. Then they are to blow up themselves—or each other—slowly until they are big, big balloons, floating around and bouncing gently off one another and off other objects. Remember, they're balloons; they must bounce very softly, as real balloons do.

Then the leader says that the air is slowly being let out of the balloons, so that once again they end up lying on the ground.

The balloons are blown up again and this time the air is released quickly, so that they shoot around the play area.

The next time the winds can come and take them for a speedy ride, or it can rain. As the weather changes (according to the leader's directions), the balloons react in different ways.

Finally, as the balloons float around, the leader shouts "Pop!" All the balloons are hit by a pin, or a tree branch; they burst and fall to the ground.

Now there are holes in the balloons, and they must be repaired by the balloon doctors, so some of the players become the doctors.

After playing this for a while, tell the players they are sticky; when they bump into another balloon, the two stick together. Soon all the players are stuck together in the largest of all balloons.

The leader can experiment with this one and take the players on some fantastic voyages.

🖎 STICKY POPCORN

Nursery school and up

All the players pretend that they are pieces of popcorn. First they act out being popped, jumping up all over the play area. Then they all become very sticky, so that when they touch another piece of popcorn they stick together. Soon everyone will be sticking together in one glorious candy-coated popcorn ball.

🪶 CATCH A MOUSE

Kindergarten through second grade

Have the players pretend that they are in a house where a mouse is loose. How would they catch it? What if the mouse were Mickey Mouse, or even Mighty Mouse? What if there were a hundred mice loose? They'd have to team up with all their friends to get rid of them all. Things can get quite hilarious with a group of children running around trying to catch imaginary mice.

🪶 TOBOGGAN

Kindergarten and up

Who says you need snow to have a toboggan ride?

About five players sit on the floor, one behind the other, holding the shoulders of the player in front of them and with his or her legs around that player's waist. Each person's only contact with the floor is his or her seat, except that the first one in line is allowed to touch hands to the floor.

Unfortunately, this toboggan does not move quite as easily or as fast as the one on snow, but it *can* be moved: Let the players see what they can do.

🪶 LIFTING IMAGINARY OBJECTS

Kindergarten and up

Here's an activity that allows even very little players to lift anything from a grain of sand to the entire earth.

Try to pick up an imaginary object. It can be something of only a few ounces, or it can weigh thousands of pounds. If it is big and heavy, the players will need the help of all their friends. They will pick up the objects together and carry them around for a while, then put them down. Have the players experiment with this newfound strength.

❧ SIGHTLESS SCULPTURE

Kindergarten and up

You will need three players for this activity: an artist, a model, and a "piece of clay." If you are ambitious, use more than one player for the model and for the clay.

The artist and the clay close their eyes. Then the model takes a pose and holds it for a few moments. Now the artist (still with closed eyes) tries to place the "clay" in the exact same position as the model. It may not turn out to be a masterpiece, but it will be fun to see what the artist can do just by feel.

❧ ROLE PLAYING

Kindergarten and up

We can all learn from role playing, but it's also fun.

Each player assumes the role of some other person, acting as they think that person would act. The idea is to use lots of imagination and really get into the role. But try to use roles that are constructive and cooperative, not critical and unkind.

❧ ELEPHANT/PALM TREE

Kindergarten and up

The group stands in a circle, with one player in the center. This player points to one of the others and says either "elephant" or "palm tree."

If "elephant," the player pointed to must become an elephant by bending over and dangling clasped hands in front of his or her head like a trunk. The two players on either side hold their arms in an oval over the elephant's head to form ears.

However, if the center player says "palm tree," the person pointed to must clasp hands and stretch his or her arms overhead. Then the players on either side hold their outer arms up and out to be leaves for the palm tree.

If someone makes a mistake, or hesitates too long, the player pointed to must exchange places with the center player.

VARIATION

Try monkey/gorilla, elephant/giraffe, or any other of your favorites.

WRING THE DISHRAG

Kindergarten and up

The players face their partner, holding both hands. Then one player brings one leg over the connected arms, and the other player does the same on the same side. The two players are now back to back and still holding hands through their legs.

Now they bring their other legs over and say "howdy" to each other—they are now once again in the starting position. They have "wrung the dishrag."

VARIATION

Facing their partner and holding one hand, the two players try to turn around without letting go. If they can accomplish this, have them try it holding both hands.

TORNADO

Kindergarten and up

Players form a standing circle. One person, the tornado, stands inside. When the game begins, the tornado goes into constant wild motion, doing anything she or he can think of. At the same time, the players in the circle change positions, crossing over to the opposite side but without touching the tornado. Those who do touch the tornado can become tornadoes themselves, or alternatively can simply continue on to their new places in the circle.

VARIATION

Try this as a scattered game, with players all over the play area rather than in a circle. Have all the players moving and trying to avoid touching the tornado. If they do touch, they, too, become tornadoes; continue until all the players are tornadoes.

❧ JAMAQUACK

Kindergarten and up

What in the world is a jamaquack? It's a bird from Australia that stands bent over holding its ankles and always travels backward. No wonder it is nearly extinct! In this game, we become jamaquacks.

To play, about half the players form a pen by holding hands in a circle. The other half are the jamaquacks. They get inside the circle, hold onto their ankles, and close their eyes. Don't forget, they can move only backward.

Once they are securely inside the pen with their eyes closed, two of the players in the circle now release their hands to form an opening in the pen. All the jamaquacks try to get out of the pen through the opening.

One thing I forgot to tell you: These birds love to talk. All through the game they say "Quack! Quack! Quack!" So when they get outside the pen, they can quack to their friends still inside in order to lead them out into the free world.

Once all the birds are out, the circle players become the jamaquacks and try their hands (or is it their ankles?) at moving in this very odd manner.

VARIATION

If very young players do not want to close their eyes or hold their ankles, play the game any way they want.

❧ CATCH THE DRAGON'S TAIL

Kindergarten and up

The players form a line, one behind the other, holding onto the waist of the player in front of them. This makes the dragon.

The player at the front of the line is the dragon's head, the players in the middle make up the dragon's belly, and the last player in line is the dragon's tail. The object of this game is for the head to catch the tail. The entire dragon must remain intact, while the head is trying to catch the tail, and the tail is trying to avoid the head. And remember: Any real dragon worth its scales makes bloodcurdling dragon noises when moving around.

VARIATIONS

Try the game with two dragons or more, trying to catch the other's tail—while keeping its own untouched.

For very young players, try holding hands or shoulders rather than waists.

🍃 SMAUG'S JEWELS

First grade and up

Needed: Handkerchief

I first played this game when I took The New Games Training sponsored by The New Games Foundation of San Francisco, where I was inspired to continue along cooperative playful ways forever and ever.

The game comes from Tolkien's fantasy *The Hobbit,* where Smaug, the dragon, was the protector of a collection of jewels. In our version one player is Smaug and kneels over a handkerchief representing the jewels.

The other players kneel in a circle around Smaug. The object of this game is for the other players to grab the jewels without being tagged by Smaug; if you are tagged you become frozen. The strategy varies; it is up to the group to work out a way to capture the jewels. The player who is successful in capturing the hoard becomes the next Smaug.

But isn't freezing the tagged players a form of elimination? Not if played the following way:

VARIATION

Have two circles, with two Smaugs and two caches of jewels. When someone is frozen, he or she simply joins the other circle. In this way, the game can go on indefinitely, and no one is ever eliminated.

🍃 SNOWBLIND

First grade and up

One player, the snowman, walks around the play area with closed eyes, singing "Snowman, snowman, all in white, Blinding everyone in sight." While the snowman is singing, the other players can move around the play area. When the singing finishes, the players stop where they are, and all of them sing the words while the snowman walks around with closed eyes.

The snowman searches for a player by listening to the singing. When he or she (because a girl can be a snowman in this game, too, of course) touches another player, that player also becomes a snowman, and must walk around with closed eyes in front of the first snowman, who holds onto the waist of the new player.

The singing resumes, and the game continues until everyone has been tagged and an entire snowman train has been formed.

✎ AMOEBA

First grade and up

An amoeba is a one-celled creature with no definite shape. It just flows along from place to place. It has a center—a nucelus; the rest is just a jellylike substance called protoplasm, surrounded by a thin cell wall.

Choose one person to be the nucleus. Three or four others—the protoplasm—hoist this person onto their shoulders. The rest of the players form a circle to be the cell wall.

The nucleus gives directions, and the whole group has to move the way the nucleus tells them to. The faster the directions come, the more fun the game is.

Be sure your players are large enough and old enough to be able to tote around the nucleus without mishap, or just play without a nucleus.

✎ COOKIE MACHINE

Second grade and up

The cookie machine is formed by two lines of players facing each other and holding the wrists of the person opposite in the other line. The players stand very close to their neighbors. The machine chants "Cook, cook, cook" continuously.

Now one player, not a part of the cookie machine, announces what kind of cookie he or she is and then jumps up and lands face down in the arms of the first pair of players in line. The players making up the machine make circular forward motions with their arms and pass the cookie along to the end and out of the machine. Be sure that the cookie stays up on the players' arms, and be gentle.

When the cookie has been "baked," someone else takes a turn to be a cookie until everyone has passed through the machine. My favorite is chocolate chip!

VARIATION

Water Bridge: This game is played at the shallow end of a swimming pool. The object is to get one player from one edge of the pool to the other without touching the water, on the arms of the cookie machine—or in this case, the water bridge. But the cookie had better have a bathing suit on, just in case.

✎ No Nukes

Third grade and up

A few players volunteer to be the power plants. They go around "contaminating" the rest of the players with a touch of their radioactive hands. When touched, players must freeze in their tracks. The only chance of freedom for the frozen players is through their free-roaming, noncontaminated friends. If two of them can encircle the frozen player and yell "No nukes!" the frozen player is once again free. But we want to get rid of that power plant. For this to be accomplished, four already contaminated and then freed players must surround the power plant and yell "No nukes!" That will mean the plant must shut down for good. If the players can do this to all the power plants, the players win. But if the power plants can contaminate everyone, the *power plants* win.

Choose Up Teams

❧ LEMONADE

All ages

One of the teachers at the school where I teach remembered playing this game as a child, so it must have been around for a long time.

Each team has a safety area at opposite ends of the playing field. The teams gather there and pick a profession or trade that they are going to pantomime, and a place that they are going to be from, such as California, New York, Chicago, etc. When they are set, the teams start walking toward one another. As they walk, the first team says, "Here we come," and the second team replies, "Where from?"

"California," they answer—or wherever they have decided to "be from."

"What's your trade?"

"Lemonade."

"Show us some if you're not afraid."

By then the teams are nose to nose and toes to toes, and the first team pantomimes the trade that they have chosen, while the second team tries to guess what it is. As soon as someone on the second team guesses correctly, the first team starts to run back to their safety area, while the other team chases them. Anyone tagged becomes a member of the second team.

Then it is the other team's turn to choose a profession and a location, and the game continues.

❧ CIRCLE TO CIRCLE

Nursery school to first grade

The group forms two circles. When the leader calls "Change," everyone changes sides to stand in a new place in the other circle. No one must touch anyone else while crossing over. For very young children, have only one circle, and have the players change places within that circle.

VARIATION

Wait a minute! Who says we can't touch? When changing, do have the players touch each other. They may even want to give each other a "5" or a handshake or a hug. Now, that's what cooperative play is all about!

🍃 LISTENING

Kindergarten and up

Divide the play area so that it has a safety zone at each end. Divide the players into two teams and designate one as the *talkers,* the others as the *rockers.* Each team lines up at the edge of its own safety area, and when the leader says "Go," they march toward one another until they are nose to nose and then stop.

Then the leader says either "I have a toy horse that . . . talks" or "I have a toy horse that . . . rocks." If " . . . talks," the talkers chase the rockers back to their safety area; any who are tagged join the other team. If the leader says " . . . rocks," the rockers do the chasing. The tagged players change teams for the next round.

🍃 REVERSE SCORING

Kindergarten and up

The following are different ways to keep score that take the "need to win" out and substitute an "all-together" approach. Some might seem a bit extreme, but they really work in practice.

Reverse Scorer: The player who scores changes sides and joins the other team if his or her side is winning. If the scorer's side is losing, no change takes place.

All Score: Everyone on the team must score before the team can claim victory.

Reverse Score: When a player scores, the score is given to the other team—as a present!

All Positions: All the players must play each position before a team can win.

Free Score: In games such as soccer or hockey, play with no goalie and make the scoring area very large. You might make an entire wall in the playing room the goal. This is a very good way for those just learning the game to play.

Backward Scoring: In games such as tennis, start the action with both sides collectively having twenty-one points. Each time a score is made, reduce the total by a point. The suspense really mounts as the players see the score approaching zero, with both teams trying not to be the one to end the game.

◎ BLOB DODGEBALL

Kindergarten and up

Needed: One or two large soft balls; several more (optional)

Four or five players, the blob, stand, holding hands, inside a circle formed by the others. The players forming the circle throw the ball at the others, trying to hit one or more of them below the waist. When this succeeds, have some of the players form a new blob.

VARIATIONS

Use two balls rather than one.

If you have a lot of players, make a very large circle and have more than one four- or five-person blob.

Have the person in the blob who gets hit with a ball join the circle players until the whole blob is absorbed into the circle.

Circle Blob: Form a smaller circle within the larger one. The outer circle throws at the inner one; every player in the inner circle who gets hit joins the larger circle.

Human Pinball (kindergarten and up): All but about six of the players form a circle facing outward. The six remaining players sit inside the circle. Using a few balls, the circle players throw them backward through their legs and try to hit the center players. When hit, that person joins the circle and becomes a thrower.

Play human pinball with the center players standing and holding hands, as in Blob Dodgeball.

❦ CROSSOVER DODGEBALL

Third grade and up

Needed: Dodgeball

Dodgeball is such a competitive game that you must wonder how we transformed it into a cooperative one. Our version is played the same way as traditional dodgeball, except that every time a player gets hit by the ball, or if the ball that is thrown is caught, that player crosses over to the other team. The object is to get all the players on one side—then everybody wins.

•

❦ MOBY DICK

Kindergarten and up

Divide your players into two groups and position them at two bases at opposite ends of the play area. Then choose one player to be the whale's waterspout. When the leader calls "Cross!" all the players cross over to the opposite base. While they are running, the leader calls out "Moby Dick!" This is the signal that the whale is spouting water, and everyone must seek safety at a base—whichever base they choose. At the same time, the waterspout tries to tag as many of the runners as possible before they reach a base. All those caught must help catch the other players when they cross the next time. The game ends when everyone has been caught and has experienced the fun of being showered at by Moby Dick's waterspout.

VARIATION

Sharks: This is the same game as Moby Dick except that the leader calls out "Jaws!" when the players are crossing, and the player doing the tagging is the shark.

❦ TUG-OF-PEACE

Kindergarten and up

Needed: Rope

Unlike its cousin by marriage, Tug-of-War, Tug-of-Peace is an activity of subtlety rather than strength. It is played with a rope, like Tug-of-War, but in our version all the players play together to keep the rope up.

Three players can form a triangle, holding a rope and keeping it off the ground at three different spots by holding it up or by placing it around their backs. Or four players can form a square with the rope. Try having the players play together with the rope in a cooperative effort by forming shapes, letters, or even figures.

❧ COOPERATIVE TUG-OF-WAR   ·

First grade and up

Needed: Rope

As in the traditional game, both teams line up on opposite sides of the rope and prepare to pull. But in this version, when one side starts to pull away, players from that side switch over to keep the game even.

VARIATION

Assign numbers to the different players on each side of the rope. When a number is called by the leader, the players on each side having that number cross over to the other side. Try to have all the players cross over before the game is finished.

Remember, all the players keep on pulling with all their strength while the crossing over is taking place.

❧ COLLECTIVE STONE

First grade and up

Needed: Bat, ball, etc.; see individual game

Here is cooperative play at its best, because in these games we take traditional sports and turn them into a fun-filled cooperative experience for everyone involved. The following format can be used for many sports—kickball, baseball, punchball, and many more.

Use as many bases as you like, not just the traditional four of baseball. After the ball is batted, in whatever manner you choose (with a bat, with the hand, with a broomstick, etc), the player who batted circles each base as he or she reaches it, rather than stepping on it.

After the ball has been fielded by one player, it is passed around the field, and every other fielder also must touch it. When the last fielder touches the ball, he or she calls "Stop!" and the runner must freeze on the spot and not start running again until the next player hits the ball. The game continues in this fashion.

VARIATIONS

Norwegian Ball: This format can be used with any game that requires hitting a ball and running around bases, but it doesn't require any bases.

After the ball is batted, the hitter's teammates form a line, and the hitter runs around them, as many times as possible, until the ball is fielded. Then it's the next player's turn. Count the number of times the hitters circle their teammates.

Rounders: In this scoring system, the team at bat hits until the number of runs scored equals the number of players on the team. Then the other team gets its chance.

Rotation: Rotate the players so that each person gets to play each position. In this way we eliminate rightfielderitis, a dreaded condition where the worst player is made to play right field.

These suggestions can be adapted to many sports, including football and soccer.

◎ NEW BASEBALL

First grade and up

Needed: Baseball or softball equipment

This new form of our national pastime is played in the same way as the traditional game except for these changes:

An out occurs whenever a ball is dropped by a fielder, whether it is a grounder or a fly.

An out is made when a grounder stops before it is fielded.

The team at bat is not retired until it has scored nine runs (one for each player on the team), so both teams must play *together* to accomplish this and allow the other team a turn at bat.

❧ BALLOON GOODMINTON

First grade and up

Needed: Balloon

Use a balloon and play badminton, having the players count together, as the teams hit the balloon back and forth. But don't hit your ball too hard, or you'll have to get a new one.

❧ CO-KICK

First grade and up

Needed: A large round ball, like a soccer ball

Players divide into two teams, and individuals on the teams pair off and are tied together at one ankle.

Set up goal areas at each end of the field.

Start play by dropping the ball in the center of the field between opposing pairs of players. The game is simply to kick the ball into the opposite team's goal area. You may or may not have a pair of players at each end defending their goal.

VARIATION

I guess this concept could be used in almost every sport or activity or game. It makes for confusion and lots of fun.

❧ SCRAMBLED EGGS

First grade and up

Needed: Several soft rubber balls

This game gets its name from the disorganized manner in which it is played!

Use as many soft rubber balls as you can find. The best playing area would be a gymnasium with a wall behind each team's side, and a middle line. Divide the players into two teams.

The players stand on their individual sides of the center, and the leader throws out the balls randomly to each team. The object is to get all the balls over to the other side by kicking, throwing, or any other means the players can come up with.

Now scramble those eggs!

❧ ROCK/PAPER/SCISSORS

Second grade and up

An old "choosing game" is turned into a cooperative running game.

The sign for a rock is a fist. The sign for paper is a fully open hand. The scissors sign is a hand with the second and third fingers pointing outward.

The order is: Rock smashes scissors; scissors cut paper; paper covers rock. Each sign can therefore beat one other sign, and each sign is vulnerable to one other sign.

There are two teams. The playing area is divided into a safety zone at each end and has a center line in the middle.

The teams huddle behind the center line and decide which sign they are going to use. Then each team approaches the center line, and at a count of three, everyone calls out, "Rock, paper, scissors" and uses the sign that was decided upon. Whichever team wins chases the other back to their safety area. Any player tagged before he or she reaches the safe line changes sides.

Now regroup with your new lineup and start the game over.

If both teams use the same sign, everyone must go back and choose a sign again.

VARIATION

Before starting, the players must decide on three signals that combine sound and movement. For example, one signal could be crossing arms across the belly and groaning; another, wiggling a fingertip up and down on the lips to make a "b-b-b-b-b" sound; a third; holding up two fingers in a "V" sign while yelling "Hooray!" The signals can be anything you choose, but be sure that all the players know them well before the game begins.

Divide the players into two teams. Each team secretly decides on one of the three signals to give. They then line up opposite one another, nose to nose and toes to toes, as close as possible. The leader says "Turn," and everyone makes a half turn so that the teams are back to back.

The leader counts to three. On "three," everyone turns around to face the other team's members and to give the agreed-upon signal.

The idea is for each team to give the same signal to one another, so if the signals given are different, the teams must huddle once again and choose a new signal to use. Keep at it until both teams are working and playing together. Then everyone is a winner.

🦋 COOPERATIVE VOLLEYBALL GAMES

Third grade and up

Needed: Volleyball equipment; Monsterball, blanket (optional)

The traditional game of volleyball has many elements of cooperation in it, but the versions listed below go beyond the regular form to make volleyball a truly cooperative experience without changing the basics of the game.

Bump and Scoot: This volleyball game is played in the same way as the traditional game, except that every time a player hits the ball over the net, she or he scoots under the net and joins the other side.

Team Bump and Scoot: Set up about four teams of four players each on each side of the net. Give names to the teams. Every time the ball is hit over the net, the player who has hit it yells his or her team's name, and *all* the players on that team scoot under the net to join the other side.

Infinity Volleyball: Here the players see how long they can keep the ball volleying in the air as they hit it from side to side. All the players collectively count how many times the ball goes over the net. Keep trying to improve the score.

Rotation Volleyball: Instead of simply rotating within one team, in this game both sides rotate together. After serving the ball, and when the team has lost the serve, the serving player goes to the middle of the other team's back line, next to their server, becoming the last server for the other side.

Collective Monsterball: Get yourself an Earthball* and together try to send it back and forth over the net.

Collective Blanketball: Get two large blankets, and give one

---

*An Earthball can be purchased from The New Games Foundation, P.O. Box 7901, San Francisco, CA 94120. It has the entire earth painted on it, so it's quite a thrill to be able to hold the world on your shoulders!

to each team. Each player grabs hold of an edge of the blanket. Together, they lift the blanket in such a way that the ball is propelled over the net to the other side, where the other team waits with their own blanket to catch it.

All-on-One-Side Volleyball: Start this game with all the players on one side of the net, and use a balloon for a ball. Each player takes a turn to tap the balloon up and over the net. As it floats over, the player who hit it ducks under the net in time to hit the balloon back and then stays on that side. But each time a player on the first side hits the balloon, he or she changes sides to hit it back. When everyone has crossed over, repeat the whole process in the other direction.

❧ TEAM BALL

Third grade and up

Needed: Large ball; Frisbee (optional)

The playing area resembles a football field. The object is for each team to move the ball to the other team's end zone by passing it from teammate to teammate. However, the player holding the ball cannot move. Only those without the ball can move and set themselves up for passes.

The team without the ball plays defense, trying to intercept the passes and recapture the ball for their team.

VARIATION

Try the same thing with a Frisbee—this is Ultimate Frisbee

Old Favorites a New Way

🪶 INDIAN CHIEF

All ages

Here is another old favorite that has survived many years and is still going strong as a cooperative, not a competitive, game.

One player is chosen by the leader to go where the others can't be seen. The other players then choose an Indian chief. The chief begins to make different movements: clapping hands; tapping himself or herself on the head, etc. The other players do as the chief does, no matter what it may be, and the chief changes actions frequently.

Now the player who left the room returns to the group and must guess who the chief is by watching what the others do.

The Indian chief becomes the next player to leave the room and guess, with the game continuing.

🪶 COOPERATIVE JACKS

All ages

Needed: Jacks, ball

Anyone who can play Jacks can play this. It is played the same way as traditional Jacks, except that the players play together instead of against one another. The first player goes for one-sies, the second for twosies, and so on until they reach whatever number they decided upon beforehand. When one player misses, everyone misses, and when one player wins, everyone wins. It certainly beats playing against each other.

VARIATION

For the young players, try it without a ball.

🪶 COOPERATIVE CHOOSING

All ages

No one likes to be chosen last, but somebody has to be, right? Wrong! Why do we have to choose at all? To make up teams? Here's the answer. Use birthdays, saying that everyone with a birthday in the first six months of the year is on one team, and the rest on the other. Or use the players' initials, with the first and the last halves of the alphabet being the deciding factors. This way is just as fair as choosing in the traditional way, and no one is ever chosen last.

VARIATIONS

Choose two leaders. Each leader chooses one player; the second player chooses a third player, and so on down the line. There *will* be a player chosen last, but each time it will be someone different, because a different person will be picking the last player each time.

I usually just let the players go to whichever team they want to start on; in most cases this turns out just fine. This is true in my games because the players always change teams within the game, as a part of the play. Let's eliminate something important for a change; let's eliminate a child's having to feel rotten.

🍃 COOPERATIVE HITTING PRACTICE

All ages

Needed: Clothesline, paper clips, whiffle balls, string; tetherball (optional)

I have invented a little hitting range where many players can practice many different sports and not worry about chasing the balls.

Baseball and Tennis Practice: Stretch a clothesline about eight feet high from the ground, between two trees or poles. Now place several paper clips on the line, evenly spaced out and not too close together; the players should be able to swing without hitting each other.

Tie a string from the paper clips long enough to reach waist high on the players. Tie a whiffle ball to the end of each string. Now we've made a hitting practice tee; when struck correctly, the ball will circle the clothesline and return for another whack by the hitter. The larger the playing area, the longer the clothesline can be, and the more players who can hit at the same time.

VARIATIONS

Golf: Lengthen the string and have the balls rest on the ground. (Then the players won't even have to yell "Fore!")

Soccer: Get a tetherball on a rope and tie it to the paper clip so the ball rests on the ground. The players can kick to their heart's content. Pelé would love it!

🖎 RING AROUND THE ROSE-Y

Nursery school

All the players hold hands while standing in a circle. Now everyone walks around and sings:

Ring around the rose-y
Pocket full of pose-y
Ashes, ashes
All fall down!

On the last word all the players fall down. Then they get up and play again.

VARIATION

Play this game in shallow water with the children. It's a great way to get the kids playing and to introduce them to getting their heads wet in an atmosphere of fun.

🖎 COOPERATIVE MUSICAL CHAIRS

Nursery school through second grade

Needed: Several chairs

The old game of musical chairs really brings out the competitor in a child. It's fight or be eliminated. In this version of the game, however, no one is ever eliminated.

Set up the chairs in the usual fashion for the traditional game of musical chairs. But you don't need any set number of chairs to start with. Whereas in the traditional game each child except the winner is systematically eliminated, in this new cooperative form no one is ever eliminated. Instead, each time the music stops and a chair is taken out, the players team up to share the remaining seats. They sit on each other's laps or share the chairs in some other way. When there are no more chairs, some of the players become the chairs and the other players sit on their friends' laps.

And there is no rule that says the chairs must be set up in the traditional line. Try scattering them about randomly.

VARIATIONS

Pileup: All the chairs are placed in a circle, with each player seated on a chair. If there are not enough chairs, have some of the players sit on other players' laps.

Now the fun begins. The leader asks a question—for example, "Do you have a sister?" Everyone who answers "Yes" moves one chair to the right. If they have to sit on someone's lap, well, that's the breaks. As more and more questions are asked there will be more and more players sharing chairs. The object of the game is to get everyone in one chair. If there are no chairs to play with, just sit on the floor, with the players sharing the same space vertically—on one another's laps!

Scramble: Place a chair or any other object in the center of the play area (you can use a mat, a circle drawn on the ground, or anything else you choose). Now set up about four teams in different parts of the play area, with each team having a name. The leader calls out one team's name—or two, three, or four of the names—and those called run to the center and touch a part of whatever it is that has been placed there.

◊ LEAPFROG

Nursery school through third grade

This is an old one, but let's expand it for more than two people.

Several players stoop in a line in a squatting position, with their heads tucked down. Now the first in a line of leapers vaults over each frog, followed by the others. At the end of the line the leaper becomes a frog, and when the last leaper has gone down the line, the end frog becomes a leaper. This continues until the frogs have turned into princes and princesses.

🐉 COOPERATIVE DUCK, DUCK, GOOSE

Nursery school through third grade

Traditional Duck, Duck, Goose is played in this way: One player walks around the seated circle of players, patting each on the head and saying "duck" as he or she does so. When the walking player says "goose" instead of "duck," the "goose" must get up and chase the tapper around the circle. If he or she is caught before going around completely, that person ends up in the "cookie jar" in the center of the circle.

In my cooperative version of this game, two players, holding hands, walk around the circle. If they are caught, the chaser joins them and they continue around the circle doing their Duck, Duck, Goose. When there are more "duckers" than people in the circle, all sit down and the game begins again with another pair of tappers.

VARIATIONS

If the "duckers" make it home before being caught, the chaser becomes the next ducker.

Try it with more than two duckers.

Instead of Duck, Duck, Goose try Spaghetti, Spaghetti, Meatball. Or Hot Dog, Hog Dog, Hamburger—or any of your players' favorites. Give the players freedom to experiment with this one; they'll love it.

Merry-Go-Round: This game was presented to me by one of my kindergarten children.

All the players form a circle, walking around and keeping the "merry-go-round" revolving. Two players run around this circle and touch one player, who then chases them back to the opening, while the merry-go-round keeps circling.

🐉 COOPERATIVE PIN THE TAIL ON THE DONKEY

Nursery school through third grade

Needed: Pin the Tail on the Donkey equipment

In the traditional game, which is always a party favorite, it is the blindfolded player's mishaps that delight those watching. In the cooperative form of this game, all the players play together to direct the person who is blindfolded. The object is to get all the donkey's tail pinned onto the right place. The onlookers shout "A little higher!" "No, no, the other way!" etc., and, playing together, everybody wins.

✏ HOT POTATO

Kindergarten and up

Needed: Ball

All the players form a circle. A ball or some other object is passed around the circle. When the leader says "hot potato," the player who is holding the ball at that point becomes the first in a separate "potato callers" circle. From then on, the potato caller or callers decide among themselves on a number to count to. When they reach that number, they all yell "Hot potato!" The player with the ball at that moment joins the potato callers. Eventually everyone will have joined the callers circle.

VARIATIONS

Start with two circles, one sitting and another standing right behind it. Everyone in the standing circle is the partner of the person in front of him or her.

The potato is passed around the seated circle. When the leader calls "Hot potato!" the player with the ball switches places with the standing partner.

Or the standing partner joins the seated partner in the inner circle.

✏ COOPERATIVE HIDE-AND-SEEK

Kindergarten and up

Sardines: This is a hide-and-seek game in reverse. Instead of one player searching for everyone else, everyone else seeks out one player. All the players but one count to one hundred with their eyes closed. While they do this, the single player finds a place to hide that is big enough to hold everyone in the game. (It might be a squeeze, but that's all right.) Then everyone searches for the hider. Each player who finds the hiding place tries to hide there too, without being seen by the others. Finally everyone will be squashed into the hiding place, just like sardines in a can.

Kat and Kittens: All the players but one are kittens. They hide, and from their hiding places they "meow." When the cat finds a kitten, that player helps the cat find the rest of the hiding kittens, until everyone is safe and found.

Beckon: In this game, all the players hide in different places, from where they can see the prison (the base). One player, the jailer, looks out and searches for the others. When the jailer finds another player, he calls out the person's name or names an article of clothing that person is wearing, and the player must come to jail.

From the jail, this player loudly calls for a "beckon" from a hiding player, who must gesture to the jailed player in order to free him or her. But if the jailer sees the free player "beckon," the free player also must go to jail. If the player is freed by a beckon, he or she tries to hide again without being seen by the jailer. The object is to get all the players into jail; if there are too many for that, have more than one jailer.

✎ Nonelimination Simon Says

Kindergarten and up

As in the traditional game of Simon Says, everyone follows the directions and actions of the leader, who is Simon, but only when he or she says "Simon Says." If these words are not spoken, the players do not follow.

In this new form of the game, two separate games go on at the same time in the play area. When one player is eliminated from a game, he or she joins the other one. This can go on forever and ever!

✎ Human Tic-Tac-Toe

Kindergarten and up

Needed: Chalk or chairs

Tic-Tac-Toe has been around for a long, long time and has been played on many boards around the world. Here the players really become part of it.

Mark a large tic-tac-toe board on the ground. (You could also use nine chairs set up to indicate the nine squares of the game.) Have the players line up. The first player in line stands anywhere on the board, either crossing arms on his or her chest to indicate an "X," or circling hands over his or her head to indicate an "O." The next player takes the opposite sign and stands in another square on the board. Each additional player alternates "X" and "O" as the game continues, until one team wins or all nine squares have been used. After the game, the players go to the end of the line and start again.

I know we end up with a winner, but there's still a lot more togetherness here than in the usual Tic-Tac-Toe game.

COOPERATIVE JUMP ROPE

Kindergarten and up

Needed: Jump rope

All the players line up except for the two who are turning the rope, and the jumper. The jumper takes a turn jumping, after which he or she changes places with one of the turners without stopping the rope. Then the next player in line takes a turn jumping, and afterward takes the other end of the rope. This continues until everyone has had a turn at each position.

This does beat fighting over who is going to turn.

COOPERATIVE TAGS

Kindergarten and up

Needed (Optional): Rolled-up newspaper; chair, stool, or box

Everyone's "It": In this game of tag, everybody is "it," but at the same time, everyone is also being chased. The object is to tag the other person before he or she tags you. Honesty is the only policy in this game, because of all the confusion of who tagged whom first.

When tagged, the player becomes frozen and he or she stands still with feet spread apart. To be defrosted, the frozen player must have another person crawl through his or her legs. (This can be changed to have the "defrosting" accomplished by a hug, a "5," a handshake, or whatever you choose. It's up to your players.)

VARIATIONS

Hug Tag: The only way to be safe in this game of tag is to be hugging someone else. Try it hugging two, three, or more players. If this gets too much for the player who is "it," just let a few friends be "it," too.

Elbow Tag: Some of the players choose partners, others are "free runners," and one or more are "it." The partners link arms at the elbow and place their outside hands on their hips, forming a link for the players running free. The free-running players are being chased by those who are "it." At any time they choose, those being chased can hook up with one of the partners' free elbows, but when this happens, the other partner must break off and run, thus becoming one of those being chased.

Hook On: This game is played the same as Elbow Tag, except that it is for very young children; it eliminates that slight degree of competition. We play this game without anyone's being "it"; all the running players do is hook onto the various free elbows, at which time the other partner then runs free.

Blob Tag: We start this game just like any traditional game of tag, with one player chasing the rest. But a funny thing happens: A blob is created! When the player who is "it" tags one of the others, they hold hands and chase the other players together. As each person is caught, she or he joins with the others, and that is how the blob is formed. The blob becomes bigger and bigger, and eventually everyone is part of it. Of course, every blob makes horrible blobbish noises as it runs around.

Try starting with two or more "its," so there will be more than one blob being formed.

Three Away: Three players hold hands, with one of these players designated as "it." Then a fourth player, the chaser, who is outside the group, tries to tag "it." The players in the group help "it" escape the chaser's tag; when "it" is finally caught, the players exchange places so that everyone gets a turn to be chaser and a turn to be "it."

Loose Caboose: Three or more players form a line, with each

holding the waist of the player in front. This represents the train. The last player in line is the caboose.

Then one player, who is not in the train, tries to tag the caboose, while everyone else tries to help the caboose evade the chaser.

Try this with many trains and many chasers.

Spoke Tag: The players form three or four lines, one end of each meeting in the middle to form the spokes of a wheel. They squat in this formation.

A single player, not in one of the lines, runs around the outside of the "wheel" and tags one of the players at the outer end of a line. This end player then tags the person in front of him or her, and the tag is passed up to the other end of the line.

When the front player is tagged, she or he gets up and runs around the outside of the wheel. This is the signal for all the players in the tagged line to run around as well. They circle the wheel until they reach their original spot.

The leader chooses another player to run around and tag a line, and the game continues.

When the players who have run around the wheel get back into line, they change their order, and the player who was in the center goes to the end.

Cops and Robbers Tag: Divide the players into two groups. Try to have more robbers than cops, but it doesn't really matter. Once the sides are set, the cops start to chase the robbers. Any robber who is caught then quickly becomes a cop. That player helps to catch the robbers who are still loose, until everyone is a cop and the world is a safer place.

There are many variations to this game, such as Shirts and Skins, Bases or No Bases, or counting to three while tagging the robbers. Try it any way your players like best.

Go Tag (kindergarten and up): All the players stand in a line, with every other player facing in the opposite direction. The two end players start off, one chasing the other around the line. Either running player can, at any moment, tag someone in the line to take his or her place, but the tagged player must start the chase in the direction he or she is facing. When one player is finally caught, the two runners take a place in line, and the new end players begin the action over again. The fun really begins when you don't know who is chasing whom!

Swat Tag (first grade and up): Every now and then it's fun to give someone a good swat. In this game one player can swat another as hard as he or she wants to, but don't worry. No one will get hurt.

The leader chooses the first player to be the swatter. The others sit in a circle. In the center of the circle is a chair with a rolled-up newspaper on it (or some other object that does not hurt when someone is hit with it; a long piece of polyethylene foam works well).

The swatter picks up the swatting piece and hits a seated player lightly on the legs with it, then runs to replace the swatting piece on the chair and return to the circle to sit in the place where the seated player had been. Meanwhile, the player who was swatted gets up, runs, and grabs hold of the swatting piece, trying to swat the first player on the legs before she or he can sit down.

If the second player manages to do this, the first player must again pick up the swatter to try someone else. However, if the first player gets back safely before being swatted, it is the second player's turn to swat someone.

Emphasize speed rather than hitting hard.

🗝 COOPERATIVE THREE DEEP

First grade and up

Needed: Ball

Form two standing circles, one inside the other. One player holds a ball in the center of the two circles.

The center player throws the ball to someone in the inner circle and immediately runs and stands behind someone in the outer circle, making it "three deep." The front player of the three goes into the center.

While this is happening, the player with the ball passes it to the person behind him or her, who throws it to the new center player. Keep this going as long as you like.

🗝 COOPERATIVE RELAYS

First grade and up

Line up half your players at one end of the play area and the other half at the other end. The first player runs and tags (gives a "5" to) the first player in the opposite line and joins the end of that line. The tagged player now races back and tags the new front player of the other line. This continues until everyone has had a chance to run. This game can be used in a hundred different ways, from passing the baton to using it on the obstacle course. Just exercise your imagination.

VARIATIONS

Over and Over: The players line up, all facing front, one behind the other, and the first player passes a ball over his or her head and back to the next in line. The ball is continuously passed backward and overhead from one to another, and after each player has passed, he or she goes to the end of the line. The game can literally go on and on. . . .

Miss Your Legs: In this form of Over and Over the ball is hiked backward through the players' legs to those behind them. Then the hiker goes to the end of the line.

Through the Loop: Your players line up. Every other player, starting with the second one, forms a loop by holding his or her arms in a circle overhead. Now the first player in line throws a ball to the third player, through the second player's loop. After throwing, both the one who threw and the "loop" go to the end of the line. Then the third player (who is now first in line) throws the ball through the loop, and so on. This continues until everyone is all looped out.

Pass It On: For this game you'll need something small and round, such as a tennis ball, an orange, or an apple. Each player must pass the object to another player in line without using hands. We might pass it tucked underneath our chin to under our neighbor's chin and on and on down the line of players.

✎ AVERAGING AND ADDING

First grade and up

Needed: Stopwatch, writing materials

In Averaging, have all the players run a set distance. Time each player, but do not stress each player's time. Instead, average all the runners' times and make a cooperative effort to improve the average the next time.

In Adding, simply add all the times together for one total score. Then try to improve on that total the next time.

VARIATION

You can use this method in many track and field events: the high jump, distance throws, even the pole vault. You can also use it in sports such as bowling or even to time how long it takes to play Octopus (page 28).

ꑼ NEW BASKETBALL

First grade and up

Needed: Basketball equipment

In this cooperative form of an old favorite we try to eliminate the dominant "big man" who is so often present in a basketball game. That's why this version of the game has different rules:

No dribbling; everyone must pass the ball.

Each player must touch the ball before a shot is attempted. In this way everyone is involved and no one stands around just watching.

No shooting from beyond the foul line—this makes the game more team-oriented.

Sometimes the players count the number of passes aloud as the ball goes from player to player.

VARIATIONS

Statues: This game helps the offensive team score and eliminates the emphasis on body contact. When the offense brings the ball up to and across half court, the defense must freeze wherever they are. Then the offensive team passes the ball from player to player and tries to score. The defense can pivot on one foot to try to prevent the score. The defense only resumes moving when they reacquire the ball, or after the offense gets a basket.

Sink It: In this version, one player attempts a shot. If successful, all the other players in turn try to make that same shot. If everyone makes the shot, the team as a whole gets an "S," the first letter in "sink it." Then the next player tries another shot. All the players keep shooting until they have spelled "sink it."

❧ RED ROVER

First grade and up

The group divides into two teams, and they stand facing each other, holding hands, from twenty-five to fifty feet apart. The leader chooses one player to be the runner, and at the call of "Red Rover, Red Rover, let [the player's name] cross over," that person tries to run through the other line.

If the try is successful, the two line players who let the runner through join the other team. However, if the runner is stopped, he or she must in turn join the opposite team.

The leader alternates runners from the two teams, and the game can continue until everyone is on the same side!

❧ COOPERATIVE BILLIARDS

First grade and up

Needed: Billiards equipment

Anyone who can play regular billiards can play this version of it. Minnesota Fats might not like this kind of pool, but I find it lots of fun.

One player shoots until he or she misses a shot; then it is the next player's turn. But unlike regular pool, in this version the players try to set up the next person for a good shot instead of trying to leave nothing to shoot at. They can set an objective, and when it is reached, everybody has won.

This is a great way for young players to learn the game without pressure.

❧ COOPERATIVE BOWLING

First grade and up

Needed: Bowling equipment

All we've done here is convert conventional bowling into a cooperative game.

The game is played and scored in the same fashion as regular bowling, except that within each frame each player throws only one ball, and the second person tries to increase the score.

In the next frame, the second player goes first. The score is taken together. If a player gets a strike, his or her partner starts the next frame.

VARIATIONS

Try bowling through your legs—or better yet, through your partner's legs.

Try it with the opposite hand.

Try it blindfolded.

Make up your own way. By playing around with the rules, the emphasis is taken off the score and placed where it belongs—on having fun!

❦ TOUCHBEE

First grade and up

Needed: Frisbee

Here's a friendly addition to the art of throwing a Frisbee.

Play catch with a Frisbee, with the rule that a player must be touching another player when he or she catches the Frisbee.

❦ ESTI WIN

Third grade and up

Needed: Stopwatch; ball (optional)

In any race I've ever seen, everyone has always been after only one thing—to finish first. In this race, finishing first takes a back seat. It's not who is the fastest, but rather those who come closest to guessing their finishing time.

Before the race, each player guesses how fast she or he will run. Then everyone tries to come as close as possible to this estimated time.

VARIATION

Try this activity with other track and field events, such as the softball throw. Just have the players guess how far they think they can throw the ball.

Something to Do

🍃 BIRTHDAY LINEUP

All ages

Have the players line up by birthday, with January birthdays first and December birthdays last—or vice versa.

🍃 MAT MADNESS

All ages

Needed: Gym mat

In this activity we use a gymnastics mat in a somewhat different way.

At least six players get under the mat and try to move it across the floor. The key is to get everyone to move in the same direction. But don't worry if the mat doesn't move at all; it's still fun just being under there.

🍃 CHORUS LINE

All ages

Have all your players line up next to one another with their arms around each other's shoulders. Now tell everyone to hop up and down. Then tell them to start kicking out their legs in unison, just like a chorus line. Try different exercises and activities from this position. They can be a lot of fun.

🍃 COOPERATIVE MURALS

All ages

Needed: Very large piece of paper; finger or poster paints

Two or more players can color a picture together, or better yet, many, many players can paint a mural. Get a very, very large piece of paper and start painting. No one has to be an experienced artist. I know it will turn out to be simply beautiful!

VARIATION

Try having the players use their feet to paint the mural. Everyone takes off shoes and socks and really gets into painting. (This way the players can paint with sole!)

❧ CATERPILLAR

All ages

Have all your players lie face down in a line as close to one another as they can, with everyone facing in the same direction. Now the first in the line rolls over the backs of the other players and lies down next to the last player. Then the next player takes a turn. This continues until the caterpillar runs out of room.

❧ COOPERATIVE SNOWPEOPLE

All ages

Needed: Snow

Did you ever think of how the snowman feels, standing there all alone? Let's give him friends, and a family, too.

The object is to build many snowpeople—an entire village of snowpeople. Build snowmoms and snowdads and even snowchildren.

Don't forget to dress warmly.

VARIATION

Try to roll the biggest snowball you ever saw. For this the players will need the help of all their friends in order to push the ball when it starts to get very big.

❧ SCHMERLTZ

All ages

Needed: One tube sock; a softball; a piece of rope

What in the world is a schmerltz? A schmerltz is a tube sock with a softball in the heel and tied at the top. To play with it, throw the schmerltz up in the air and try to catch it by the knot. Or have a catch with your friends. Maybe one day we'll have a Schmerltz World Series.

VARIATION

A bola is a schmerltz with a long rope tied at the top of the sock. Form a standing circle with one player in the center holding the end of the rope. This player spins the rope around so that the bola circles a few inches off the ground. The players in the circle must jump over it as it passes by them. As everyone gets better at jumping over the bola, lift it a little bit higher. Take turns spinning the rope.

❧ NAME STAMP

Nursery school and kindergarten

With the players standing in a circle, each person takes a turn to say his or her name and then stamps one time for each syllable. Find out whose names have the same pattern of stamps and have them do it together.

❧ MUSICAL HUGS

Nursery school and kindergarten

Needed: Music

Start the music and have all your players move randomly around the play area. When the music stops, everyone must hug someone else. That's all there is to it. Then start the music again, and whenever it stops have three, four, or more players hug together in a great big hug. It's a great way for your players to get to know their neighbors.

❧ MOVE TO WORDS

Nursery school and kindergarten

Spread out the players in the play area. The leader says a word and all the players react and move to it in any way they want. The leader can choose any word: sad, happy, mad, scared, glue, or even "supercalifragilisticexpialidocious." Or the leader can simply make up a word. The players can move with their friends or alone.

✒ DANCE FREEZE

Nursery school and kindergarten

Needed: Music

Play some lively music. When it is being played the players dance around; when the music stops, all the players must freeze. The leader can have groups of two, three, or more players freeze together.

✒ CHOCOLATE PUDDING

Nursery school and kindergarten

Get the players together in a group. Tell them they are a bowl of chocolate pudding and that someone is shaking the bowl. All together the players shake the way they think the dessert would. The shaking stops, and slowly the pudding stops jiggling, but not for long. Once again, at a signal from the leader, it starts to shake.

VARIATION

Vibrating: Just have the players stand together with their friends and vibrate all their muscles. It's a great relaxer—as though kids that age need one!

✒ TOUCH BLUE

Nursery school and kindergarten

When the leader says "Touch blue," all the players must touch something blue, either on someone else or in the play area. Then the leader may say "Touch knee," and everyone must touch someone else's knee. Continue to name things for the players to touch.

VARIATION

When the players touch one thing, have them keep holding on to that as the leader gives them the next instruction. They may get a bit twisted, but that's just added fun.

❧ HUGS

Nursery school and kindergarten

Needed: Music (optional)

The players run around the play area, doing whatever they feel like. When the leader shouts "Hug!" each player finds someone to hug. Then the leader says "Go!" and the players are off on their own once again.

The next time have three, four, or more players hug together.

VARIATION

This can be done to music, with the players running when the music is being played and hugging when it stops.

❧ MAT SLIDE

Nursery school and kindergarten

Needed: Two gym mats; flight of steps

Here's a good way to make an instant slide. All you need is a couple of gym mats and a staircase.

Place one gym mat over a flight of steps and another at the bottom of the stairs for protection from falls. The players run up the mat and then slide down it.

Try having them walk down very slowly, resisting the force of gravity.

To make it really tough, have them try it in their socks. This way they'll really have to rely on their friends to help them get to the top of the mountain.

❧ MERGING CIRCLES

Nursery school through first grade

The players are scattered around the play area in small groups, holding hands to make circles. Each circle moves throughout the play area, circling about, trying not to bump into any other. If two circles do collide, they merge into one larger one. You keep playing until there is just one huge circle with everyone included, and then you can play some circle games with your newly formed large circle.

VARIATION

This is played indoors. The players form a circle, holding hands, and walk in one direction until their circle reaches a wall. When this happens, the circle gently rolls along the wall, each player, in turn, touching the wall with his or her back. It's a great way to move together.

TWISTER

Nursery school through first grade

The leader tells the players to get into some strange position and hold it as they attempt a second move. For example: "Put your nose on someone else's leg below the knee. Now put one hand against the wall."

And so on. How long this continues depends on the leader's inventiveness and how limber the players are. Sooner or later they'll fall over—and laugh!

WHAT DO YOU SEE FIRST?

Nursery school through first grade

All the players close their eyes and simply experience the darkness. Then they open their eyes and each player shares with the group what he or she "saw" with eyes closed, and what was the first thing the player saw when opening his or her eyes.

COOPERATIVE SAUCERS

Nursery school through second grade

Needed: Chair

This activity originated at the school where I teach when a group of nursery school kids started to spin one child around while he sat in his seat. When we did this we used a plastic seat that had no arms, but a secure chair will do. One player sits in the chair, and as many other players as possible give that lucky person a ride up and down and all around. Let everyone have a chance to take a ride.

❧ DOE DOE DEE DEE

Nursery school through second grade

Here's a game that sounds a bit silly and complicated—but it's not. It's great fun. If you chant "Doe doe dee dee" six times and then end with "Yum, yum," it's sure to make your food taste better.

Everyone, including the leader, is seated in a circle, Indian style—with legs crossed—and very close to his or her neighbor. They sing "Doe, doe, dee, dee" six times. During the first time, the players hit their thighs with the palms of their hands. On the second, they cross their arms and hit left palm to right thigh, right palm to left thigh. The third time, they touch right hand to the right-hand neighbor's leg; the fourth, left hand to the left-hand neighbor's leg.

Now it gets tough. On the fifth repetition of "Doe, doe, dee, dee," the players touch their left hand to their nose and their right hand to their right ear. On the final repetition, they cross their left hand to their right ear and their right hand to their nose. Finish with "Yum, yum," as all the players rub their stomach.

VARIATIONS

The players place their arms around their neighbors' shoulders and sway from side to side while singing the verse.

For younger players, just do one or two of the hand movements. Or make up some other movements of your own.

Kids have told me that their food tastes better after a good "Doe, doe, dee, dee'—especially hot dogs.

After a while, let the kids play alone, without the leader.

❧ PLAYING IN SILENCE

Kindergarten and up

The players do whatever they are doing, but they do it in silence. No talking, please. You will be amazed at what other forms of communication they will come up with and how they can communicate without talking.

🖎 FEATHER BLOW

Kindergarten and up

Needed: Feathers

The object of this activity is to keep the feathers up in the air and off the ground by blowing. Just pucker up and blow, and keep the feathers flying. (If the players really want a challenge, try this one in a chicken coop.)

🖎 JUMPING OVER HANDS

Kindergarten and up

Players line up behind one another facing front. The first two bend over and hold hands so that the other players in line behind them can jump over their arms. After everyone has jumped, these two join the end of the line and the next two form the barrier to be jumped. Continue at least until everyone has had a chance to be jumped over.

🖎 SPOKES

Kindergarten and up

All the players stand sideways in a circle, as close as possible to their neighbors and one behind the other. The circle should be small enough so that all the players can hold hands in the center. They reach into the circle with their inside hand, so that everyone's hand is touching. With their outside hand, the players point outward. Now all the spokes are set for a ride. Try to keep the wheel intact while moving in a circle.

✎ SQUEEZE

Kindergarten and up

Needed: Several rocks or big stones; chalk; shells, nuts, marshmallows (optional)

Collect a large number of rocks or big stones—several for each player. Draw the outline of a circle, a person, a square, or other shape on the ground. One player at a time places a rock within the diagram, but not on any lines and not touching any other rocks. See how many rocks the players can get within the picture. If a rock touches another rock or a line, it is taken out and placed into the dead rock pile, or simply taken out and tried again later (or just leave them in, touching the other rocks or the lines).

VARIATIONS

Try this activity at the beach, using shells in the sand.

Squirrel: This variation is fun, because we use nuts, and when we are through playing, we eat the "equipment."

Draw a small circle on the ground. Now each player gets a handful of nuts. Standing upright, one player at a time tries to drop a nut into the circle without its bouncing out. At the end, all the players share those nuts that remain inside the circle.

Try it with rocks or marshmallows. Throw away the rocks; eat the marshmallows.

✎ HAMMERS AWAY

Kindergarten and up

Needed: Board, nails, hammer

The first player (or the leader, if the player can't do it) gives the nail a good, secure whack into the board to start the action. Each player in turn then hits the nail one time until finally it is driven into the board all the way.

See how few hits it can be done with. Then start all over again with another nail.

🍂 PEOPLE PYRAMIDS

Kindergarten and up

It's best to have the heavier players on the bottom, but that's not always the most fun. Try it any way the players like it best.

For a ten-player pyramid, four players kneel in a line, as close to one another as possible. Three more players kneel on the first four's backs, two more kneel on top of these. The last player either kneels, or if she or he is very daring, stands on the top of the pyramid. (I hate to say it, but be careful.) Now collapse.

🍂 LAP GAME

Kindergarten and up

All the players stand in a circle, facing in. The leader then says "Right" or "Left," and every player takes a ninety-degree turn in that direction, to end up facing the next one's back.

At the signal of "On your knees, please," everyone bends knees, making a lap, and sits on the lap of the player in back of him or her. If done properly, the circle will support itself. It might be a bit tough if your players are of varying heights, but falling down is fun, too.

Then the circle stands again, faces in the other direction, and sits this time on the other neighbor's lap.

Also, the entire circle of players could spread their arms and be airplanes, each leaning way back on the next player. Be sure that all the players are close together for this game.

(The record, as reported by *The New Games Book*, is 1,468 cooperative players all in a circle!)

🍂 QUICK LINEUP

Kindergarten and up

It is very important in this game to watch and listen to the leader.

Divide the players into four teams, with each lining up near a different wall. The four teams are set up to form a square, facing in.

The leader stands in the center of the square. These are the positions the teams will be in in relation to the leader every time the action stops. When everyone is set, the leader turns around in place several times. When he or she stops turning, each team must then reposition itself near another wall so as to end up in the same relation to the leader as it was originally—in front of, in back of, to the right of, or to the left of the leader.

The object is for everyone to get back in place as fast as possible. Sounds hectic? Just try it.

VARIATION

If you think your players can do it, have them line up in order of their height or their birthdays.

⊠ SINGING COMPLAINTS

Kindergarten and up

Too many things that people complain about are nonsense. Let's let them complain, but only if the complaint is sung. Let all the people with the same problem get together and sing their complaint. Soon their problems will not seem so important.

⊠ SKIN THE SNAKE

First grade and up

Everyone stands in a line behind one another. Now, with their left hands, the players reach between their legs and grab the right hands of the players in back of them. Everyone does this at the same time. Then the last player in line lies down on his or her back, and the person in front of this player backs up, straddling the one on the ground, and lies down behind him or her. Don't forget to keep holding hands. One by one the entire line does this. Once everyone is lying down, reverse the process. Have each player get up in turn, still holding hands. Congratulate your players. They have just skinned a snake!

Once up again, have them try walking while still holding hands.

❧ CARRY ON

First grade and up

One player lies on the ground, face down and stiff as a board, with arms out straight. Three other players pick the player up, two by the arms and one by the legs. They carry their friend as far as they can.

❧ JIGSAWING

First grade and up

Here is a great way for the players to discover new games with their friends. They put a game together as they would a puzzle.

Each player is given one piece of information to the same new game—one they have never played before. All get together and exchange information. Afterward, all the players play the game they have just learned.

FOR EXAMPLE:

A What?

Give each player one of the following clues:

The group sits in a circle.

You'll need an object—a ball, a shoe, a stick, or something else easy to handle.

Pass the object around the circle from player to player.

The person passing the object says "This is a dog" to the one receiving it.

The player receiving the object says "A what?" and the passer repeats "This is a dog."

As the object is passed, the questions and answers must be passed back each time to the first player.

Try passing one object (a "dog") one way around the circle and another (a "cat") in the opposite direction at the same time.

❧ SHARING THE LOAD

First grade and up

The object of this activity is to transport everyone from one side of the playing area to the other, but each player must be carried across, except the very last player, who can walk.

As many players as are needed to carry a friend across to the other side of the play area, leave him or her there, and return to the original side. Continue this until everyone has been carried across except the last player, who can cross over alone to the triumphant cheers of his or her fellow players. See how fast the players can accomplish all this.

Who's Got a Ball?

❧ PASS AND CATCH

All ages

Needed: Ball

Form two parallel lines facing each other. The first player in one line tosses a ball to the first player in the other. Once the ball is thrown, the player runs to the end of the other line. Now the player who has caught the ball tosses it to the next one in the other line. As each person throws, he or she runs to the end of the opposite line. The game continues, with everyone getting a turn to throw as well as catch.

VARIATIONS

Triangle: Three players form a triangle, standing a short distance apart. One player throws the ball to a neighbor, who catches it with one hand and throws it with the other. Each player in the triangle gets a turn to catch and throw as the ball goes around and around.

Try it with four players making a square, or with more players making whatever figure you wish.

One player stands in the center of the circle and throws the ball to anyone standing in the circle. Then this player throws the ball back to the center player. Continue this until everyone has had a turn. Then pick a new center player. Do not make the circle too large in this game, for then too many players will have a long wait for a turn.

❧ BALL MADNESS

Kindergarten and up

Needed: Several balls

Using as many balls as possible, pass them all around the circle at the same time in either direction, to everyone's total confusion and delight. Pass them slowly or pass them fast, but pass them—and have a ball!

❧ LAP BALL

Kindergarten and up

Needed: Ball

The circle of players are seated very close to each other, shoulder to shoulder. The object is to pass a ball around the circle from lap to lap without using hands. The younger players are allowed a friendly hand if it is needed.

❧ NAME PASSING

Kindergarten and up

Needed: Ball

The players pass a ball around the circle. As each player passes the ball, he or she must call out the name of the neighbor to whom the ball is being given. The players continue calling out names as they move the ball around the circle.

VARIATION

Have the players sit in a circle and roll the ball to someone else, not necessarily to the next person, still calling out the name of the player to whom it is being rolled.

❧ JUMPING BEAN

Kindergarten and up

Needed: Balls, sheet or old bedspread

We need a large piece of sturdy material, such as a sheet or an old bedspread. We have to cut a hole in the center, so make sure the material is old.

Everyone takes hold of the material at the edges. We put one or more balls on the material and together lift it up and bring it down so that the ball or balls are jumping up and down like jumping beans. Now try to get the ball or balls to go through the hole.

🍂 FOX AND SQUIRREL

Kindergarten and up

Needed: Two balls

The group stands in a circle and passes a ball, the fox, around the circle. Seems simple enough, right? But now we bring in the sly squirrel, another ball that can be *thrown* around the circle in any direction the players choose. The object of this game is for the fox to catch the squirrel, which he does when one player is in possession of both the fox ball and the squirrel ball at the same time. Remember, the fox must be passed from neighbor to neighbor, while the squirrel can be thrown anywhere in the circle. When the squirrel is caught, start over.

🍂 CIRCLE BALL

Kindergarten and up

Needed: Ball

Players form two separate circles. One player in the first circle throws the ball toward the second and calls out the name of one of the people in it. That player tries to catch the ball as it is thrown. Then that player calls out the name of a player in the first circle, throwing the ball toward him or her. Keep throwing the ball back and forth as the names are called.

VARIATION

Try this game with three or more circles while giving each circle a name. Then the thrower must call out the name of the circle as well as the name of the player who is to catch the ball.

🍂 THE BALL GOES ROUND AND ROUND

Nursery school and kindergarten

Needed: Balls

Here we have a cooperative version of a good old game. In the traditional form, a ball is passed around the circle and this verse is sung by everyone:

The ball goes round and round
It stops at every town
And when it stops it stops at
Y-O-U!

Then whoever is holding the ball at the end is eliminated.

But there's a better way. Just keep playing the game with no elimination. Start with two equal circles fairly close together, and when the ball in each circle goes round and round, have the eliminated players join the opposite circle. This way play continues with no one forced to sit and watch; there is total participation.

✍ Alphabet Ball

Nursery school through third grade

Needed: Ball; other objects, such as a shoe (optional)

Pass a ball around the circle. As each player passes it, he or she says a letter. Go through the alphabet this way.

VARIATIONS

Pass any object, from a shoe to a person. Say the letters together as a group.

Cooperative Counting: Start counting, with each player saying a number in turn. Go as high as possible.

Try to count in unison.

✍ Roof Ball

First grade and up

Needed: Rubber ball or tennis ball

Get a rubber ball (or a tennis ball), some friends, and a roof. One player throws the ball up onto the roof; the next tries to catch the ball when it reappears. Try it with one player being the thrower, the next jumping over the ball as it lands, and the third catching it on one bounce. Let each player have a turn at each position.

❧ SAME PASS

First grade and up

Needed: Ball

The players form a circle, and a ball is thrown around, not necessarily to a player's neighbor. The players must remember to whom they threw the ball, because every time they get it after that, they must throw it to the same person. Make sure no two players throw to the same person, so everyone can be involved in the game.

❧ PING-PONG TOSS

First grade and up

Needed: Ping-Pong ball, cardboard tube, ring(optional)

The players toss a Ping-Pong ball back and forth, trying to catch it with the cardboard tube that had held aluminum foil, waxed paper, or even toilet tissue. It's harder this way, but also much fun.

VARIATION

Try tossing a ring back and forth from one player to another, catching it on a stick.

❧ FOX CHASE SHEEP

First grade and up

Needed: Softball

One player is the fox and has a ball. All the other players are the sheep, and they run away from the sly fox. When the fox tags a player with the ball, that player becomes a frozen fox and must freeze in position. The fox does *not throw* the ball at the running sheep, but just tags them. But the fox can throw it to another player, who catches it and becomes a fox, too. The fox with the ball is the only one who can tag the sheep.

The object is to change all the sheep into foxes.

Guess What!

✎ TRY TO REMEMBER

Kindergarten and up

This is a game that requires a good memory, but if your memory is as bad as mine, don't worry. Your friends will help you.

Have all the players but one form a circle; the single player stands in the center. All the players must try to remember the order in which the circle players are standing.

Now break the circle and go on to some other activity for a short period. Then have the center player try to put the others back into the original order. The other players help if necessary. After the circle is reformed, make a new one, with a different player in the center. Again take some time off and then let the new center player—with help from all the others—try to put the players back in order.

✎ HIDDEN MOVEMENTS

Kindergarten and up

Two players leave the play area, and the others decide on an activity for the absent players to do. For example, the activity could be sitting on the ground facing one another, holding hands, and pulling one another back and forth.

The absent players return and try to discover what the activity is. They do different things, and the group responds with different levels of applause, foot stamping, cheering, or any means *other than talking* to tell them whether they are hot or cold. When the activity is finally guessed, everyone breaks out into loud sounds of approval.

✎ DO YOU HEAR A NOISE?

Kindergarten and up

Needed: Small bell or other small noisemaker

One player sits in the center of a circle with closed eyes. The circle of players pass the bell around, each player ringing it once, and then stop it and put their hands behind their backs. The center player opens his or her eyes and tries to guess where the bell was when it stopped ringing.

❧ COOPERATIVE PANTOMIMING

Kindergarten and up

Chain Pantomime: All but one player leaves the room. The one player left decides on an act to pantomime. Then the leader calls one other player back into the room, and the pantomime is acted out for him or her. Another player is called back, and the second person acts out the pantomime. This continues until all the players, one at a time, have returned to the room, have seen the pantomime, and have acted it out. The final player acts out the pantomime and then tries to guess what it is.

I'm Thinking of a Word That Rhymes With . . .: A player picks a word—for our demonstration, the word will be "play." Then she or he says "I'm thinking of a word that rhymes with clay" (or any word that rhymes with "play"). The other players take turns acting out what word they think it is. As they act out their words, everyone else tries to guess what it is. If they act out the correct word, they start over. However, if the word they are acting out is the wrong one—"day," for instance—the leader says "No, the word I'm thinking of is not 'day.' " The players keep acting out their guesses until they hit on the correct word, with the other players getting their clues from their friends' pantomimes.

❧ PSYCHIC SHAKE

Kindergarten and up

Count off by ones, twos, or threes. Then everyone walks around the play area, shaking hands with whomever they meet. If your number is "one," you shake the other player's hand once. If your number is "two," you shake two times, and if your number is "three," you shake three times. The confrontation comes when *different* numbers meet and shake, because each player will be shaking a different number of times. One player will want to stop shaking while the other player will want to continue. The object is to find the players with the same number. When these do meet, they become "psychic teammates" and proceed through the game together, looking for other players with the same number. The game ends with everyone in his or her number group—all psyched out. (Remind the players not to talk.)

VARIATION

Use this game to form teams, simply varying the highest number in each according to the number of teams needed.

☙ Tin Man

Kindergarten and up

Needed: Paper heart

The Tin Man in *The Wizard of Oz* made it clear that everyone needs a heart. Here's a game that takes care of the need.

The leader gives half the players a piece of paper to indicate a heart (or Valentine-style hearts can be cut out of red paper). All the players move around the play area with eyes closed. Players who have a heart say "dub"; those who need a heart say "lub." When a dub meets a lub, a heart is exchanged.

☙ Slot Machine

Kindergarten and up

The leader divides the players into three different groups and assigns each group an activity to pantomime. One group could act out the Statue of Liberty, for instance, in whatever way the players in the group decide upon. Another could act out Niagara Falls, the third the first flight of the SST. It doesn't matter what, as long as each group does a different pantomime.

Now all three groups pantomime their acts at the same time. Then each group becomes familiar with the others' pantomimes by having each acted out separately.

Now each group huddles alone to decide which one of the three actions they are going to pantomime. When the leader places an imaginary quarter in an imaginary slot machine and pulls the lever, all three groups act out at the same time the pantomime that they chose. If all three are the same, the leader wins the jackpot; if the pantomimes are different, the leader loses the quarter and must play again.

Keep playing until the leader has only enough money left for the bus ride home—or until she or he is very wealthy.

🍃 GOTCHA!

First grade and up

In this game, the players use the football ploy of faking a pass to try to fool the guesser. A small object, like a marble or a stone, is passed around the circle and one player, standing in the center, tries to guess where it is. The deception comes into play when some players fake a pass when they really aren't holding anything.

Pass the object from hand to hand in a way that no one can see it and no one really knows where it is except those doing the passing.

VARIATION

Try it with the players standing in a line, with the guesser standing in front of the passers.

🍃 PRUI

First grade and up

All the players close their eyes and start walking around the play area. The leader silently taps one player on the head; that player is Prui, who now stands still with eyes open.

When one person bumps into another, they ask one another "Prui?" If they hear "Prui" in return, they know they have not found Prui, because the real Prui can't talk.

When the question is "Prui?" and there is no reply at all, the asking player knows that he or she has found the right one; the reward is to take Prui's hand and open his or her eyes. Once a player is on the Prui line, he or she cannot talk, however. As the line grows, each player who, with eyes closed, encounters it must feel his or her way to one end of the line before holding hands opening his or her eyes. Finally all the players are on the Prui line.

✎ TREASURE HUNT

Third grade and up

The leader writes simple clues, prepared in advance, on slips of paper and hides them. (To make it more complicated for older players, the leader can tear each clue in two pieces and hide the pieces.) The players try to find the clues and put them back together so they can use them to find the treasure. (I usually use a watermelon as the treasure so everyone can share it at the end and then take part in a vigorous pit spit—after they have eaten the evidence.)

What'll We Play Now?

❧ So Fa Game

All ages

The children of China have many cooperative games. Here is just one of them.

Half the players form a circle. The other half skip around inside the circle of friends, clapping their hands. When the leader says to do so, each player inside the circle runs up to someone in the circle and plays a quick patty-cake game with him or her. Then all the players clap their hands, spin around, shake hands with their partners, and exchange places. The game continues from the beginning once again.

❧ Ha Ha

All ages

All you have to know for this activity is how to lie down and how to laugh.

One player lies on his or her back on the ground. The next player lies at a right angle to the first, with his or her head on the first player's stomach, and so on, each player at right angles to the one before.

Continue this until everyone is lying on someone else's stomach, with every other player parallel.

Now the first player says "ha," the second player says "ha ha," the third player says "ha ha ha"—and the fifteenth player says fifteen "ha's." If the players lose count and simply break into uncontrollable laughter, it's perfectly all right. That's what it's all about.

❧ Shoe Biz

All ages

Each player removes one shoe and places it in a pile in the center of a circle. Then each player takes a shoe and gets back in place. Everyone holds hands but still keeps hold of the shoe. At this point the players try to return the shoes to their owners without letting go of their neighbor's hand.

VARIATION

Try exchanging other pieces of clothing, such as jackets.

⚘ BLUEBIRD, BLUEBIRD THROUGH MY WINDOW

All ages

Select one player who will be the bluebird. The others form a circle, holding hands and raising them up high to make an arch between each pair of players. The bluebird flies around, weaving in and out of the circle, passing in front of every other player. As the bluebird flies, everyone sings:

> Bluebird, bluebird through my window
> Bluebird, bluebird through my window
> Bluebird, bluebird through my window
> Oh, Johnny, I am tired.

At this point, the bluebird stops and stands behind the nearest player in the circle, tapping him or her on the shoulder. Now everybody sings:

> Take a little girl [boy] and tap her [him] on the shoulder
> Take a little girl [boy] and tap her [him] on the shoulder
> Take a little girl [boy] and tap her [him] on the shoulder
> Oh, Johnny, I am tired.

The player who was tapped then gets in front of the first bluebird, who holds him or her on the shoulders, and both weave in and out of the circle while everyone sings the first verse again. When the verse is finished, they both stop behind a player, and the game continues, with the third player joining the front of the train after the singing is over. As the game goes on, the circle gets smaller and smaller and the train gets longer and longer until everyone has joined the train.

VARIATION

Try having everyone clap hands while they sing the second verse.

🌱 SMILE IF YOU LOVE ME

All ages

Telling someone not to smile is like telling an elephant not to eat peanuts. It's impossible for anyone to do—but it's lots of fun trying.

Everyone stands in a circle, with one player in the middle. That player steps up to one of those in the circle, looks the person right in the eye, and says, "Smile if you love me."

The other player answers, "I love you, but I can't smile." If this player cannot keep from smiling, he or she must enter the circle and join the first player in trying to make the others smile.

The players might have to try very hard to come up with their funniest faces to make the last "hardhearted" person smile. But the game should end with everyone smiling and giggling with delight.

🌱 GET DOWN

All ages

With everyone in a standing circle, the leader enters the circle and starts to move to the verse below while singing it:

Jump up, chew-chi-chew, chew-chi-chew, chew-chi-chew
  [jumping and pointing hands up]
Jump down, chew-chi-chew, chew-chi-chew,
  chew-chi-chew [squatting and pointing down]
Jump left, chew-chi-chew, chew-chi-chew, chew-chi-chew
  [pointing left]
Jump right, chew-chi-chew, chew-chi-chew,
  chew-chi-chew [pointing right]

After really getting into this singing and movement, the leader walks up to one of the other players in the circle and says "Hey, there! You're a real cool cat! You've got a lot of this and a lot of that! So come on in and get down."

The selected player enters the circle with the leader and they repeat the entire chew-chi-chew verse, with everyone else joining in the singing. When the song is finished, both players in the middle approach different circle players with the "cool cat" verse and have them join in the center.

The group sings the song again, and then these four invite four more players to join them inside the circle. The game goes on and on until everyone is in the middle singing and really "getting down."

❧ COME ALONG

Nursery school and kindergarten

One player is chosen to walk around a circle of all the others and choose different players to "come along." As the players are picked, they hold hands and walk around together. At some unspecified time, the leader says "Go home," and everyone who is on the line finds a place to sit in the circle. Then the game continues with new players walking around.

❧ HOWDY, PARTNER!

Nursery school and kindergarten

This game is a favorite in my nursery school classes.

One player is chosen to run around the circle of seated players and pat someone on the head. The player who is patted rises and runs in the opposite direction. When the two meet, they stop, shake hands, and say "Howdy, partner!" Then the first player runs and sits down, while the other person pats someone else on the head and the game continues.

VARIATION

If you have a large group, play with two or more doing the patting, instead of having everyone just sitting and waiting for a turn. This way more people are involved in the action.

❧ SEWING UP THE GAPS

Nursery school and kindergarten

All the players but one stand in a circle with their arms at their sides. That one player runs into and out of the circle. Every time that person passes between two circle players, those two join hands to "sew up" the gaps. Soon the entire circle will be holding hands.

🖋 ELBOW-NOSE REVERSE

Nursery school and kindergarten

The first player turns to the person next to him or her, points to his or her elbow, and says, "This is my nose." The second player does the same to the neighbor on the other side, and the game goes around the circle. When it reaches the first player again, that person sends another confusing message. That's all there is to it.

🖋 MOVING TO SOUNDS

Nursery school and kindergarten

This game is good for players who are just learning the alphabet. It helps them to memorize their ABCs and have fun as well.

All the players hold hands in a circle. The leader chooses a letter sound, such as "tuh" for the letter T or "buh" for the letter B—any sound for any letter in the alphabet. The players start walking around the circle as the leader says different words. When the players hear the particular letter sound the leader has chosen, they sit down. After everyone has sat down, they all stand up and the game continues with a different letter sound.

VARIATION

Try having different players take turns saying the various words as they walk around.

🖋 UP AND DOWN AND ALL AROUND

Nursery school through first grade

We all walk around on our two feet, but there are other parts of the body that could support us.

This activity starts by the players running around the play area singing "Up and down and all around." Then the leader calls "Freeze!" and a number. If the number is, for example, three, then all the players must stop and touch the floor with three body parts—possibly two feet and one hand. Then the leader says "Melt!" and the players move around again, singing "Up and down and all around." "Freeze eight" could mean five fingers, two hands, and one foot, or any other combination of eight that each player chooses.

VARIATION

When the leader calls "Freeze!" have the players pair up with partners; in combination they will put down the specified number of body parts.

It's great at a count of "Freeze two" to watch one player standing on one foot and helping a partner do a headstand by holding his or her feet.

🍃 Do You Like Your Neighbors?

Nursery school through second grade

One player in the circle is asked by the leader "Do you like your neighbors?" If the answer is "Yes, I like my neighbors," then everyone in the circle changes place to form a new circle of friends. If the answer is "I like my neighbors, but I want some new ones now" the player names two other players to be his or her new neighbors, and the two old neighbors change seats with the two new ones.

🍃 Cat and Mouse

Kindergarten and up

The players stand in a circle holding hands.

Two players are chosen by the leader to be the cat and the mouse. They stand outside the circle. As usual, the cat chases the mouse. But the circle helps the mouse to escape by lifting their arms up whenever the mouse wants either to enter or leave the circle, and by lowering their arms when the cat tries to follow.

When the cat manages to catch the mouse—or at any other suitable time—switch cat and mouse roles among the players to allow others a chance to run.

VARIATION

High Windows: This game is played the same way as Cat and Mouse, except that there are no names for the runners and the hand-holding circle makes the windows, which are raised and lowered when the players run through.

✿ CLOCK

Kindergarten and up

All the players hold hands and stand in a circle. Then they start moving clockwise, faster and faster, until each player is back to where he or she started. Then everyone runs in the opposite direction. See how fast the players can go without letting go.

VARIATION

Try circling one way until the group is too dizzy to stand. Then everyone sits down and thinks about going in the opposite direction.

✿ STRING ME ALONG

Kindergarten and up

Needed: Spoon, ball of string

Have all the players stand in a line, shoulder to shoulder. The first player takes a long piece of string, tied to a spoon, and passes it up his or her left arm, through his or her clothes, and down the right leg. The next player takes the same end of the string and passes it up the left pants leg (or up the left leg) and out the right arm through the shirt sleeve. This continues until everyone is tied together, using the least amount of string possible. Then the last player in line gently pulls the end of the string to free everyone, and all the players get a strange sensation when the string passes along their bodies under their clothing. It can be fun to be strung along.

✿ FROZEN BEAN BAGS

Kindergarten and up

Needed: Bean bag for each player

All the players balance a bean bag on their heads and move around the play area. If the bean bag falls off, the player is frozen and cannot move. To be defrosted, another player must pick up the fallen bean bag and place it back on top of the player's head, while keeping the bean bag on his or her own head. If it falls off while the player is attempting to help a friend, the helpful player is frozen and the player he or she is trying to help remains frozen.

🖾 ISLANDS

Kindergarten and up

Needed: Frisbee, plate, or similar object

We start with a Frisbee or some other object (or more than one). Put the object on the ground. The players move around the play area. When the leader gives the signal, the players try to touch the Frisbee without touching anyone else. See how many players can touch the same Frisbee without touching the other players.

VARIATION

Wait a minute! Why should touching be forbidden? Let's try it now with everybody touching each other. Ah! Now, that's more like cooperative play!

The leader sets down a piece of cloth or newspaper, and all the players try to crowd onto it. That's all there is to it. The smaller the cloth in relation to the number of players, the more difficult—and more fun—it is to do.

🖾 KNOCK YOUR SOCKS OFF

Kindergarten and up

This game should be played on a soft surface, such as a mat or grassy area on which a playing area, not too large, has been marked off. The players remove their shoes and kneel. The object is to get the other players' socks off. (Remind everyone to pull straight and gently, to avoid twisted ankles.)

❧ UNSMILING

Kindergarten and up

Two lines of players face each other; their object is to get one player at a time to laugh. The first person starts the long walk between the two lines with a straight face. The players in the two lines must get that straight-faced player to crack a smile but may not touch him or her. The poker-faced player must look at the players in the line, and they can do any silly thing to make that gloomy person smile.

❧ GROUP THUMB WRESTLING

Kindergarten and up

Thumb wrestling has been a sport for a very long time and is basically competitive. But when a circle of players wrestles with two partners at the same time, within a circle of other wrestlers, it comes out to be cooperative. It really doesn't matter who wins; everyone is having so much fun.

Any even number of players can participate. They stand in a circle, every other player with crossed arms, each holding both neighbors' hands in the traditional thumb-wrestling position. Now everyone wrestles, but be careful of that thumb on the other side of you!

❧ STREETS AND ALLEYS

Kindergarten and up

Let's assume we have twenty-seven players, although any number can play. Have all but two of the players form lines of five, holding the hand of the person next to them. The lines should be arm's length apart. The other two players are chaser and "chasee." (Of course, you will adjust the number of players in the lines according to how many are in your group, but try to form even lines if possible.)

The "streets" are formed by the players' arms.

Now one of the two remaining players chases the other. They run up and down the lines formed between the players' arms. When the leader (or, if you choose, the chaser) calls out "alleys," the players in line let go of their neighbors' hands, make a right turn, and again hold hands with their new neighbors, changing the "streets" to "alleys." At any time during the game the word "streets" or "alleys" changes the position of the players in line. When the line is forming new streets or alleys, the players running simply freeze where they are until the leader shouts the word "go."

The chaser cannot reach across the streets or alleys but must catch up with the other runner. If this sounds complicated, don't let it deter you; the confusion is half the fun.

🔖 THAR'S A B'AR

Kindergarten and up

All the players form a line, standing one behind the other. Then the first player turns to the second player and says "Thar's a b'ar." The second player responds by saying "Whar?" The first player then points straight ahead and says "Over thar." The second and third players repeat this conversation, with the second player pointing in the same direction as the first player did. Continue this until the entire line is standing and pointing.

Then the first player starts again, with "Thar's another b'ar." The second player again says "Whar?" but this time "Over thar" is pointed out with the other hand. Now each player ends up pointing with both hands.

Now the first player says "Thar's a tiny, tiny b'ar." When the second player asks "Whar?" the first crouches down in a squatting position and points with his or her chin. Again the words and actions are passed along the line. But this time everyone is shoulder to shoulder, crouched down with both arms and chin pointing.

Now the clincher! The first player says "Thar's a *great big* b'ar," and when the second asks "Whar?" the first points with a shoulder, leaning on the second player. When this is passed along the line, everyone usually ends up like one of a line of dominoes—falling down on his or her neighbor.

❧ How Do We Look? How Do We Sound?

Kindergarten and up

How many of us ever really get the opportunity to see how we look to others? This game gives us all the chance.

With everyone standing in a circle, the leader takes a few steps toward the center of the circle and says his or her name, at the same time acting out a movement, possibly accompanied by noises. If it were my turn, I would take a few steps into the circle and say "Jeff," and maybe I would raise my right fist high and bring it down fast while grunting out loud.

After I did that, the entire circle of players would re-create what I had just finished doing so I could see how I looked. Then it would be someone else's turn, until everyone had a chance to see themselves as others see—and hear—them.

❧ A What?

Kindergarten and up

Needed: Any small object, such as a pebble, a bean bag, etc.

This game is as confusing as it is fun. Half the enjoyment is in trying to remember whom to talk to and what to say.

An object is passed around the circle. The first player passing it names it (anything will do), saying, for example, "This is a dog."

The game then proceeds like this:

Second player: "A what?"
First player: "A dog."
Second player (passing on the object): "This is a dog."
Third player: "A what?"
Second player (turning to the first player): "A what?"
First player: "A dog."
Second player (to the third player): "A dog."

Each time, the statement must go back to the first player. Continue this until the object has gone around the entire circle.

VARIATION

Pass "a dog" one way around the circle and "a cat" in the opposite direction. When both objects meet and pass each other, the fun—and confusion—*really* begin!

🦢 NUMBERS AND NAMES

First grade and up

The players count off around the circle until everyone has a number. Then one player starts by saying someone else's number. Without hesitating, the player whose number was called says someone else's number. This continues until someone hesitates. Then the game is started over.

Young children can use their names instead of numbers.

VARIATION

To add a little excitement to this game, the player who hesitates when it is his or her turn could be required to do a Caterpillar (see page 72) over all the players' backs. Or choose your own penalty, but please make it cooperative.

You can also play this game in a line instead of in a circle.

🦢 LIFT MEE, LIFT WEE

First grade and up

In this activity, one person is lifted a few inches off the ground by another and then let down. If the one player can't manage this, a third player helps out. Then those who were lifted and those who lifted join together to be lifted by the next team of players. It doesn't matter how many people it takes to lift one; use as many as are needed, but try to accomplish it with as few as possible.

If necessary, have some of the players volunteer to switch sides to help in the lifting.

❧ BOARD AND SPAGHETTI

First grade and up

Two players face each other, with a third standing between them. The middle player makes his or her body stiff as a board. Both end players touch the center one gently, and slowly push back and forth. Then, as confidence is built, the end players move farther apart. When everyone feels very confident, let the center player stand with eyes closed and fall into the arms of the two others.

For "spaghetti," the center player is very loose, like a strand of cooked spaghetti. See what the two end players can do with their friend. For instance, they can try picking the center player off the floor with no assistance from him or her. Switch places after a while so everyone gets a chance at all positions. After the players have finished this activity and have built up a big appetite, go out and have a bowl of spaghetti!

VARIATION

Players choose partners. They stand facing one another at about arm's length apart, extend their arms, hands palms out, and lean toward one another until their hands touch. Then they push back against the partner's hands until they are upright again. Repeat this, moving farther and farther apart each time.

❧ PLAYER PASS

First grade and up

About six players form a small circle, standing very close to each other so that there is barely any room between the players. One player stands in the center. The center player very slowly starts to fall, but members of the circle catch this person and pass him or her, leaning, around the circle.

Start with the circle very close to the center player. As confidence is gained, increase the distance from the center. Take turns so that everyone gets a chance to be the faller. When the center player has total confidence in the others, it's time to try falling with closed eyes.

🐾 TRAFFIC JAM

First grade and up

Needed: Chalk or pebbles

Draw a series of squares in a line on the floor with chalk, or mark them off on the ground with pebbles. In the center of the line, leave a blank space. The players take their places in the squares, one side of the line facing the other across the blank space. The object of the game is for all the players on one side of the free spot to change places with all on the other by moving into the free spot one at a time. No one may move backward. Players can either move forward or jump over the one in front to reach the unoccupied space. The game is a bit like leapfrog, but with an objective.

🐾 BUMPITY BUMP BUMP

First grade and up

The players stand in a circle with one person in the center. Each player on the circle learns the names of those on each side. The center player then points to one of the circle players and says either "Left bumpity bump bump" or "Right bumpity bump bump." The player pointed to must say the name of the person at whichever side has been asked for. If the circle player comes up with the right name before the center player says the last "bump," the games goes on as before. But if the circle player forgets, or finishes the name after the final "bump," that player switches with the person in the center, and the game continues with a new center player.

VARIATIONS

Say "Hickey pickey hokey pokey doo dad" instead of "Bumpity bump bump."

Try your own tongue twister.

◎ ZEN CLAP

First grade and up

A "Zen clap" is a one-handed clap; obviously it makes very little noise.

The group sits in a circle, and one player begins the game by placing a hand flat on the top of his or her head and saying "yin." That hand is pointing to the left or right (depending on which hand is used). Whichever neighbor is pointed to puts a hand under his or her chin, with fingers pointing to someone else in the circle, and says "yang."

The third person—the one pointed to—extends an arm, pointing to anyone else in the circle, and says—nothing. (That's the silent clap.)

The player whom the third person has pointed to begins again with hand on head, saying "yin," and the sequence repeats. Start slowly and see how fast you can go. When everyone is thoroughly confused, stop, take a deep breath, and start all over.

Let's Play Quietly

❧ REFLECTIVE LISTENING STORYTELLING

All ages

One player starts a story by saying a few words. The next player continues where the first one left off. The third player picks up from the second, and so on. Keep it up until the story is fully told and everyone has had a turn.

VARIATION

One-word story: Each player says just one word until the story is told.

❧ RAIN

All ages

This game is quite simple. All each player does is repeat whatever the player to his or her right does.

Everyone sits perfectly still and quiet in the circle, with closed eyes, waiting for the leader's first movement. The rain slowly starts as the leader rubs his or her palms together. When the player on the leader's left hears this sound, he or she makes it, too, and each person starts upon hearing the player to the right. (It might be helpful for each person to nudge the neighbor on the left as he or she starts the movement.)

Once everyone is rubbing palms, the leader increases the sound of the rain by snapping fingers, and that sound in turn is passed around the circle.

For the next round, the leader claps both hands together, and that sound, too, is passed around the circle. By this time, the rain is really starting to come down. The leader then switches to thigh slapping, and the finale of the storm comes with feet stomping as the rain reaches hurricane proportions.

Now the storm will start to subside. The leader reverses the order, beginning with thigh slapping, then hand clapping, finger snapping, palm rubbing, and finally passes around *silence* as the storm dies away.

Don't forget that during all of this the players have their eyes closed. We have taken everyone through an exciting weather trip and brought them home safely.

❧ YARN FIGURES

All ages

Needed: Small pieces of yarn; ball of yarn or string (optional)

Give each small group of players a supply of different pieces of yarn in various colors. The first player puts one piece down on the floor. The next player adds another to the picture. This continues until all the yarn is used up and there is a yarn picture, which I'm sure will be beautiful.

VARIATIONS

Give one player a ball of yarn or a ball of string to unravel on the floor, making a design out of it. After a short time, the next player takes over, and this continues until the ball is used up and everyone has had an artistic hand in the masterpiece.

Try it with a roll of toilet paper.

Have all the players sit in a circle, and pass the toilet paper around the circle as it unravels in everyone's lap.

❧ RELAXING

All ages

Have all the players lie down together and pretend they are sleeping. Have them snore, or do anything else they want to help them have fun and relax.

This is a great activity after an active game or at the end of a play session. It will calm everyone down.

❧ THE MORE WE PLAY TOGETHER

Nursery school

With the group sitting in a circle, have each player place his or her arms around the shoulders of the neighbors on either side. Now everyone sways from side to side and sings:

The more we play together, together, together
The more we play together, the happier we'll be.
For my friends are your friends, and your friends are my
    friends.
The more we play together, the happier we'll be.

VARIATIONS

Try running and holding hands while singing the song.

Sing it while doing anything, anywhere. The fun is doing it together.

❧ THIS IS MY FRIEND

Nursery school and kindergarten

The players sit in a tight circle. The first player turns to the neighbor on one side, asks his or her name, takes that person's hand, holds it up high, and says, "This is my friend Johnny (or whatever). The second player then repeats this with the neighbor on the other side. The action goes all around the circle until all the players have been introduced and are holding hands. All together, the whole circle gives a cheer and falls backward.

VARIATION

Have the players use made-up names, like "Cinderella" or "Winnie-the-Pooh." Kids love to do this. If you have a large circle, start the game going in two separate directions at the same time, as in "A What?"

❧ RHYTHM CLAP

Nursery school through first grade

We each have our own rhythm, but the aim of this game is for all the players to end up rhythmically together. Everyone starts to clap until everyone is clapping together. The rhythm will be changing continuously, but don't let that throw the players off.

❧ TOUCH ME

Nursery school and up

In this activity, two players sit close enough so they can touch. As the leader calls out different parts of the body, the players touch each other there.

VARIATION

Try this activity with more than one partner and have the players use both hands. Or touch with feet, knees, elbows, or any other body parts possible.

✍ TELEPHONE

Kindergarten and up

This is an old game, and always a favorite.

With everyone seated in a circle, one person whispers a simple statement to his or her neighbor, who in turn whispers it to the next player. The statement is passed all around the circle, until it gets back to the beginning. The player who last hears it says it out loud.

You'll find there is quite a difference between what was first whispered and what the group ends up with.

✍ BUZZ

Kindergarten and up

Here's a real oldie that is a great game when the players are sitting quietly, especially on long car rides.

The players take turns counting one number at a time, but whenever a player is supposed to say a number with seven in it, he or she says "buzz" instead. If a player forgets and says "seven" (or "seventeen," or "twenty-seven," etc.), then everyone starts over again from one. The toughest part comes when you reach the seventies. See how high the players can get.

VARIATIONS

Try using multiples of the number seven, as well. In this form, there would be "buzz" for fourteen and twenty-one as well as for seven and seventeen.

When the players get very good at it, try Bizz Buzz, where the "bizz" is for threes and the "buzz" for sevens.

Try Bizz Bang Buzz, using different numbers, to make it more and more challenging.

❧ SOUND STORIES

Kindergarten and up

Anyone can tell a story, but it takes a real imagination to tell one using no words—only sounds that make no sense at all.

One player or more close their eyes and another makes a sound, either by mouth or by slapping or hitting himself or herself or something else. The player with closed eyes gives a name to the sound—and both players then make up a story to go along with the sounds they have just played with.

❧ SINGING SYLLABLES

Kindergarten and up

One player leaves the room, and the rest of the group decides on a word to sing. If the word is "cucumber," for example, some players will sing "cu-cu-cu," some will sing "cum-cum-cum" and the rest will sing "ber-ber-ber," all at the same time.

Now the player who left the room returns and tries to figure out what the word is. Everyone gets a turn to be guesser, with, of course, a new word sung each time.

❧ WATER CUP PASS

Kindergarten and up

Needed: Paper or plastic cup with water

This is a great game for a hot summer afternoon, when all everyone wants is to jump into a swimming pool—but all you have is a cup of cold water!

Standing in a circle, the players pass a cup of water around—without using their hands. The cup is passed from mouth to mouth. If some water spills—well, so much the better.

❧ COOPERATIVE CARD GAMES

First grade and up

Most card games, ideal for quiet-time activity, are competitive. Even in solitaire the player plays against the house. Here are card games that are played cooperatively.

Heaven: Cards are dealt equally to each player (any extras are discarded). Dealing out one card at a time in turn, the player with the highest card takes that trick. Before play starts, each player guesses how many tricks he or she will take; if each player has guessed correctly, everyone has won!

Sequences: Sit in a circle and deal out all the cards—with several players, you can use more than one deck. The object is to get runs of four cards in number sequence, regardless of suit. The players arrange their cards in numerical order and put down any four-card runs they may have. Then, at a signal from the leader, each player simultaneously calls out a card they may need to complete a run still in their hand, and any other player who has that card passes it to the left. At the same time the other players pass a card they don't need to the left as well. It is up to the individual player to pluck his or her card from the offerings as they come by.

Then players put down any runs they may have made receiving the new cards, and again everyone calls out another card they need, and the passing goes on again.

Players may add cards at either end of the run, once the initial four-card run is down. When everyone's cards are in runs in front of them, the game is over.

Trades: You will need at least several decks of playing cards for this game. Shuffle all the cards together and deal each player about seven or more, depending on how you are playing.

Each player looks to see what the suit is of the highest card in the hand. If it's a tie, the player chooses one. Then all the players with high cards of the same suit form groups in different parts of the room. The object of this game is for each group of players to get all the cards of the same suit. They place their cards on the ground in order, from ace to king (ace counts as one in this game). If there are any duplicates, they hold them in their hands.

Now the players circulate around the room, asking for cards that their own team needs to complete the run. They trade for these cards. They can trade only cards that are the same number but a different suit, or cards that add up to the same number. So a five of diamonds can be traded for a five of spades, and a three, four, and ace of one suit can be traded for an eight of another suit. If your team gets duplicates in a trade, they must be traded away.

The game is over when each team has a run in its own suit. Then any duplicates can be discarded.

VARIATION

This game also can be played with a "fate box"—a pile of the extra cards not needed. The players can swap cards with the fate box, or they can simply discard their extras in it.

❧ COOPERATIVE CHECKERS

Anyone who can play regular checkers can play these games

Needed: Checkerboard, checkers; Chinese Checkers equipment

Both players try to exchange their pieces with the other player's pieces on the opposite side of the board. The game is won when all the checkers are in the reverse order of the way they were at the beginning of the game. In this version, we play with no jumping, but you could always change the rules.

Chinese Checkers: This game is played in the same way as the traditional game except that the object is for the players to place their last marble in their own home area on the very last move. All the players try to finish the game at the same time, and everyone wins.

❧ POLITE CONVERSATION

First grade and up

Two players are given totally different phrases by the leader, with neither knowing what the other's phrase is. Then these two players hold a conversation, trying to work in their given phrase without the other realizing what it is. The phrases can be anything from "The Giants won the pennant" to "The rain in

Spain falls mainly on the plain." Make up some real doozies and have fun.

🔊 DICTIONARY

Third grade and up

One player picks a strange word from the dictionary and writes down its definition. All the others then make up their own definitions for that word, going by what it sounds like to them. They write the definitions on separate pieces of paper, which are then mixed up. The definitions are read aloud, and everyone tries to guess which they think is the original one. Try to pick words that no one in the group has ever heard.

VARIATION

Have the players also guess who provided which definition.

For the Few or the Many

🌱 FREE RIDE

All ages

Needed: Board with wheels or skateboard (optional)

One player gets down on the floor and the others pull him or her for a free ride. The kids love this. Let them have fun while the leader watches, or have the kids pull the leader for a while.

VARIATIONS

Cooperative Scooters: Five people play together. Get a board with wheels under it (or a skateboard). One player lies down on the board, and each of the remaining four players takes an arm or a leg and pulls the friend around the play area. Let each player have a chance to get a ride as well as to help give one.

Try this with one player sitting on the board and a few others pushing or pulling.

🌱 COOPERATIVE MASSAGE

All ages

Have everyone face in the same direction after making a circle. Each player then places his or her hands on the shoulders of the player in front and gives that person a firm massage—and a good back scratch. Now swing around and give the neighbor on the other side the same treatment. Not only are we getting a good massage, we're giving one at the same time.

🌱 PASS THE MASK

All ages

With everyone sitting in a circle, one player turns to the next, looks right into his or her eyes, and makes a funny face. The second player passes on the face to the third, and so on around the circle. At the same time, the first player has turned to the person on the other side and made a different funny face, which is passed around in the other direction. Continue until both "masks" have reached the first player again, or until laughter has stopped the game.

VARIATIONS

Pass a "5" in one direction and a hug in the other. (My three-year-olds start hugging everyone in sight every time I mention passing a hug.)

Pass funny sounds, like "zoom" and "zerk."

❧ HOW DO YOU DO, SHOE?

All ages

All the players take off their shoes and sit in a circle with the shoes in front of them. At the leader's signal, they begin to pass the shoes around the circle. Whenever the leader calls "Change," the passing switches to the other direction. When the leader calls "Find," players must be on the lookout for their own shoes, and as they get them, they keep them and continue passing the others, until everyone has his or her shoes back again.

❧ BALLOONS UP

All ages

Needed: Balloons, not blown up

Blow up a bunch of balloons. Then rest! Now everyone try to hit them in the air and keep them going up, up, and up, all at the same time.

VARIATIONS

Get the Point: Give everyone a fairly sharp pencil. The players must try to keep the balloons up in the air by hitting them with the pencil point. Good luck!

Dying Balloons: You'll need a room full of balloons and a room full of players. The players try to keep all the balloons up in the air because any balloon that touches the floor must be "put to sleep" by being stepped on. It's painful, but it's the only way! Let's hope the balloon doesn't become an endangered species.

❧ HOOPLA

All ages

Needed: Hula hoops

Put from two to twenty-two players inside one hula hoop. They then try to move either forward, backward, or from side to side. The idea is that the players have to play together to get anywhere. Try it with a lot of players; put many hoops around them at one time.

❧ JACK-IN-THE BOX NAME GAME

Nursery school

One player starts by saying the name of his or her neighbor. As the name is spoken, that player jumps up and quickly sits down again, just like a jack-in-the-box. Then this second player says the name of his or her neighbor on the other side, and that player jumps up. This continues around the circle until everyone has had a turn to be a jumping jack.

VARIATION

The leader says different players' names, and as their names are called they quickly jump up and sit down again.

❧ NAME MOVERS

Nursery school and kindergarten

With the players in a circle, the first person says his or her name, accompanying each syllable with a different movement. For instance, I might say "Jeff-" and at the same time stamp one foot. Then I would say "-rey" for the second syllable of my first name, and here I might clap my hands. I would do my last name the same way. Then the group as a whole repeats the name, with the same movements. Everyone in the circle gets a turn. It's a great way to get acquainted, or to remember names.

VARIATION

Itch: One player in the circle addresses the next, saying, "My name is Mary [or whatever the player's name is] and I itch here," touching a spot on her or his body. The second player then says, "You are Mary and you itch here," showing where Mary itches on her or his own body. The second player than turns to the third, says her or his own name, and shows where her or his itch is. This continues until everyone has met-and itched!

🐍 SNAKE

Kindergarten and up

This is a game in which the players start to spread out but eventually end up on top of the action and really together.

All the players stand in a line, holding hands. The player at one end stands still and the one at the other end slowly leads the line around him or her. As the line snakes around, it gets harder and harder to move, and more and more players must stop circling. Finally no one is able to move any more, until two very cooperative players raise their linked hands to allow the line to pass under and unwind itself.

🐍 GROUP LEAN

Kindergarten and up

Have the players form a circle and count off by twos. With everyone holding hands, have the "ones" lean forward and the "twos" lean backward. Then reverse the direction in which the players lean. Experiment with having different players lean different ways, always counting on their partners for support.

🐍 TANGLING

Kindergarten and up

For this activity, as many players as possible, from two to a hundred and two, get tangled together, using their arms, legs, and the rest of their bodies. Then comes the hard part—which is where the fun really begins. The players must try to untangle themselves. That's all there is to it.

VARIATION

Select a few players to stay out of the group, and then to try and separate it by gently tugging and pulling until the whole knot starts to come apart.

🌱 CIRCLE PASSING

Kindergarten and up

The players sit in a circle with their legs straight out in front of them and touching the legs of their neighbors on either side. Everyone's feet nearly meet in the center. A single player stands in the center, touching everyone else's feet with his or her own.

The center player then slowly falls into the lap of one of the others, and slowly, the players in the circle roll this person over the outstretched legs. Make sure everyone has a turn.

🌱 MODELING

Kindergarten and up

The players use their bodies to form sculptures by lying on the floor with one another. Their bodies can be touching, overlapping, over or under, any way. They can build numbers, shapes, animals, monsters, even electric people machines. Let everyone use his or her imagination. Players can even stand up with others leaning on them. There are no rules for this activity except having fun.

🌱 DROP IT

Kindergarten and up

Needed: Marble or other small object

Have several players line up next to one another, facing forward, with their hands palms up in back of them. Another player walks in back of them and drops a marble (or other small object) into one of the players' hand. This player then jumps forward and tries to run to a specified area without being touched by the others in line. Then another player is chosen to drop the marble, and the game continues.

❧ How Many?

Kindergarten and up

This is a good way to help beginners learn numbers.

The players begin by running around the play area. When the leader says a number, the players form groups of that number of players, holding onto one another.

When the leader says "Go," the players run around again until a different number is called.

❧ Knots

Kindergarten and up

Here is an activity that really ties people together.

At least five players stand in a small circle and place their right hands out in front of them, thumbs up. With the left hand, each grabs someone else's thumb, but not that of anyone next to him or her. The object of this activity is to untangle this knot by stepping over, crawling under, or turning around, anything is permitted except letting go. If the players really get into a dead-end situation, they can always apply "knot aid"—allowing one player to let go and untangle, after which they all join hands again. But don't let them give up too easily; most knots can be untangled with a little patience and plenty of together-ness.

Don't let two players grab one another's hands, or all that the two will do is stand around and get in the way as everyone else tries to untangle the knot.

❧ Clocks

Kindergarten through second grade

Here is an activity that is fun and can help children who are learning to tell time.

The players play together randomly. When the leader calls out a time, the players show that time by lining up like the hands of a clock. Use as many players as you wish. If there are a lot, they can form a circle with the hands of the clock inside the circle, or one player can stand in the position of each number.

🗡 THE LAST ACT

All ages

This is always the very last activity of the day. It has been called many things in the past, but the most popular name for it is "cleaning up."

In The Last Act, everyone pitches in and cleans up the play area. See how many pieces of paper or other trash the players can come up with. Don't allow anyone to escape this activity.

✒ BIBLIOGRAPHY

Aronson, Elliot. *Social Animal.* San Francisco: W. H. Freeman, 1978.

Deacove, Jim. *Games Manual of Non-Competitive Games.* Perth, Ont., Canada: Jim Deacove, 1974.

———*Cooperative Games Manual Supplement.* Perth, Ont., Canada: Jim Deacove, 1978.

———*Sports Manual of Co-Operative Recreation.* Perth, Ont., Canada: Jim Deacove, 1978.

De Koven, Bernard. *The Well-Played Game: A Player's Philosophy.* Garden City, N.Y.: Anchor Books/Doubleday, 1978.

Fluegelman, Andrew. *The New Games Book.* Garden City, N.Y.: Dolphin Books/Doubleday, 1976.

———*More New Games.* Garden City, N.Y.: Dolphin Books/Doubleday, 1981

Csikszentmihalyi, Mihaly. *Beyond Boredom and Anxiety.* San Francisco: Jossey-Bass, 1975.

Harris, Frank. *Games.* Philadelphia: Frank Harris, 1976.

Harrison, Marta. *For the Fun of It.* Philadelphia: Philadelphia Yearly Meeting of the Religious Society of Friends, Peace Committee, 1975.

Huizinga, Johan. *Homo Ludens: A Study of the Play Element in Culture.* Boston: Beacon Press, 1950.

Jones, Ron. *The Acorn People.* New York: Bantam Books, 1976.

King, Nancy. *Giving Form to Feeling.* New York: Drama Book Specialists (Publishers), 1975.

Lentz, Theo, and Cornelius, Ruth. *All Together: A Manual of Cooperative Games.* St. Louis: Peace Research Laboratory, 1950.

Leonard, George. *The Ultimate Athlete.* New York: The Viking Press, 1975.

Magill, Richard A., Ash, Michael J., and Smoll, Frank L. *Children in Sport.* Champaign, Ill: Human Kinetics Publishers, 1978.

Martens, Rainer. *Joy and Sadness in Children's Sports.* Champaign, IL: Human Kinetics Publishers, 1978.

Michaelis, Bill, and Michaelis, Dolores. *Learning Through Noncompetitive Play Activities.* Palo Alto, Calif.: Education Today Co., 1977.

Orlick, Terry. *The Cooperative Sports and Games Book.* New York: Pantheon Books, 1978.

————*Winning Through Cooperation.* Washington, D. C.: Acropolis Books, 1978.————and Botterill, Cal. *Every Kid Can Win.* Chicago: Nelson Hall, 1975.

Piers, Maria W., and Landau, Genevieve Millet. *The Gift of Play.* New York: Walker and Company, 1980.

Rohnke, Karl. *Cowstails and Cobras.* Hamilton, Mass.: Project Adventure, 1977.

Schneider, Tom. *Everybody's A Winner.* Boston: Little, Brown & Co., 1976.

Selye, Hans. *Stress Without Distress.* Philadelphia: Lippincott, 1974.

Torbert, Marianne. *Follow Me.* Englewood Cliffs, N.J.: Prentice-Hall, 1980.

Tutko, Thomas, and Bruns, William. *Winning Is Everything and Other American Myths.* New York: Macmillan, 1976.

Van Tassel, Katrina, and Greimann, Millie. *Creative Dramatization.* New York: Macmillan, 1973.

❧AGE LEVEL INDEX

First Grade and Up

Second Grade and Up

Third Grade and Up

◙ INDEX OF GAMES